JOEY'S STORY

A PORTRAIT OF A SCHOOL LEADER

JOSEPH P. BATORY

A SCARECROWEDUCATION BOOK

The Scarecrow Press, Inc.
Lanham, Maryland, and London
2002

A SCARECROWEDUCATION BOOK

Published in the United States of America
by Scarecrow Press, Inc.
A Member of the Rowman & Littlefield Publishing Group
4720 Boston Way, Lanham, Maryland 20706
www.scarecroweducation.com

4 Pleydell Gardens, Folkestone
Kent CT20 2DN, England

Copyright © 2002 by Joseph P. Batory

All rights reserved. No part of this publication may be reproduced, stored in a retrieval system, or transmitted in any form or by any means, electronic, mechanical, photocopying, recording, or otherwise, without the prior permission of the publisher.

British Library Cataloguing in Publication Information Available

Library of Congress Cataloging-in-Publication Data Available
Batory, Joseph P. (Joseph Patrick)
    Joey's story : a portrait of a school leader / Joseph P. Batory.
      p. cm.
    "A ScarecrowEducation book."
    Includes bibliographical references.
    ISBN 978-0-8108-4420-9

    1. Batory, Joseph P. (Joseph Patrick) 2. School superintendents—Pennsylvania—Biography. I. Title.

LA2317.B28 A32 2002
371.2'011'092—dc21

2002005763

©™ The paper used in this publication meets the minimum requirements of American National Standard for Information Sciences—Permanence of Paper for Printed Library Materials, ANSI/NISO Z39.48-1992.
Manufactured in the United States of America.

"It says in the Bible, when there is no vision, the people perish. And I think a really great school administrator needs a profound sense of justice to prevail."

—Jonathan Kozol

CONTENTS

Foreword — vii
Prologue — 1

1. The Bully — 3
2. It's All about Dreams — 9
3. Reflections on My Work in Camden City — 13
4. My Life in Academia — 21
5. Community Turmoil — 27
6. Back into the Fray — 33
7. Personnel Adventures — 37
8. A Stroke of Fate — 43
9. Philosophy Drives Leadership — 45
10. The Visibility Factor — 49
11. About School Boards and Food — 55
12. The Arranged Marriage — 59
13. A Visit from the FBI — 61

CONTENTS

14	My Students	65
15	The Slush Fund	71
16	The Silence of the Shepherds	75
17	The Insanity Speech	81
18	The Private Sector and the Schools	85
19	The Moral Vacuum	89
20	An Author Unpublished	97

Epilogue	101
A Summary of the Messages of This Book	105
Bibliography	107
About the Author	109

FOREWORD

This book is about the twists and turns and the uncertain directions of life. Its focus is on the evolution of a very successful educational leader. It traces his early difficulties of growing up in a large city. It then highlights a series of unlikely events and influential mentors that shaped this leader's philosophies of education and life. It documents his surprising ascent to the superintendency. And finally, it summarizes much of what this leader did when he was at the top for fourteen years. All of this is a very personal account. The narrative is candid, angry, passionate, tender, and, at times, even funny. It is also filled with poignant messages.

What you are about to read is not some typical academic treatise on educational administration. It contains no prescriptions for managerial success. Rather, it is the unusual life story of a very unique school leader.

This book hits hard at the core beliefs, the complexities, the strategies, the politics, and the moral issues surrounding public education in America. In that sense, it is not just for sitting or would-be school leaders, but also for every citizen who cares about schooling in the United States.

PROLOGUE

The cold darkness of a damp, winter day loomed outside the classroom window. Joey had been practicing his part of a duet piano piece he would play with his sister at the school's annual Performance Day in two weeks. It was 5:00 P.M. and Joey was frazzled. He felt like a trapped rat! By 3:30 P.M., all of the other kids had scrambled out of the parish school to play in the slushy snow that blanketed the neighborhood. But Joey had been forced into rehearsing on this stupid piano for the last hour and a half. Worse yet, he was laboring under the piercing eyes of the ill-tempered Sister Ignatius.

This nun had an interesting teaching technique. Every time Joey hit a wrong key (which was not infrequently), Sister Ignatius would grunt unintelligibly and pound his fingers with a wooden three-foot-long pointer. Joey's eyes were filled with tears. His ten-year-old fingers ached with pain. In his mind, he cursed his overseer and vowed to give up the piano forever just as soon as he was big enough to tell her off! Joey wanted to be with his good friends, Sal and Rocco, who were waiting for him outside the school. He couldn't wait to get away from the clutches of this volatile nun and join his buddies.

Joey made another mistake on the piano. The pointer cracked down on his fingers. Sister Ignatius called him a snot-nosed idiot. How much of this could any human being take?

Joey leaped off the piano bench. He bravely stood and barked in the nun's face: "I'm not takin' your crap anymore. I quit, you worthless old witch!" Sister

PROLOGUE

Ignatius responded by wildly swinging her pointer like a baseball bat at Joey's head. Joey ducked under the slashing stick and sprinted for the school's front door with the nun in hot pursuit. He burst into the cold air like a bullet. He was running for his life. As the irate nun followed him out the door, she was stopped in her tracks by two well-aimed snowballs from the outside darkness that immediately smashed into her bulky body.

The coatless Joey and his snowball throwing saviors, Sal and Rocco, escaped into the wintry night. They heard the angry threats of Sister Ignatius calling after them. Joey figured he was as good as dead!

The telephone call from the convent arrived at his home before Joey did. He was sent to bed without any dinner. Sister Ignatius thankfully left out lots of the more colorful details of the confrontation in talking to Joey's mother, but disrespect at school was not something tolerated by his parents. Joey was informed by his father that he would have to apologize to his brutal nun tormentor. He would also be staying after school to clean toilets and urinals for the next two weeks. Finally, yet another edict from his mother informed Joey that he would definitely be playing that piano duet with his sister in two weeks, or else!

Life for Joey was truly bad before his outburst against Sister Ignatius. But now it got much worse! In subsequent weeks, Joey was degraded, beaten, humiliated, and endlessly terrorized as the hopeless captive of Sister Ignatius.

1

THE BULLY

There were more than a few crazy aspects of growing up in southwest Philadelphia in the 1950s, but none as absurd as just getting to high school. In my heavily Catholic, working-class area, all of the students going on to the designated archdiocesan high school from our local parishes had to utilize public transportation. And on our trolley or bus rides leaving our community each day, hundreds of us white kids would pass by hundreds of black kids coming in the other direction from their neighborhood situated around the large Catholic high school where we white kids were headed. Meanwhile, the black students were going to a public high school right smack in the middle of the mostly white neighborhood we were leaving. It was all very bizarre, one very segregated society—a not-so-pretty sign of the times.

At fourteen years of age, as much as I despised the prospect of the daily public transportation adventure to high school each day, I was delighted in ninth grade to have finally escaped the nuns and their arbitrary behavior. I quickly learned that the Christian Brothers who ran the high school were much more fair. Basically, in their modus operandi, students only got whacked for doing something wrong. What a wonderful concept. I thought that I had died and gone to heaven! Who knows? I might even enjoy school. And then, only two weeks into my high school experience, I met Hiraldi.

Hiraldi was a small-time street punk who looked like the rodent he was. He was a master at spotting the vulnerable. I was one of that species, just a

CHAPTER 1

loner guy from a small Catholic parish trying to mind his own business. And I didn't have enough expertise in handling rodents. I became one of Hiraldi's favorite targets.

At first, it was simple stuff. Hiraldi would get in my face inside the school. With four or five of his goons looking on, he would make a show of knocking all my books and notebooks out of my hands and then he would stomp everything into the floor. Most of the time, I just stood there scared to death as Hiraldi roared with laughter.

On other occasions, Hiraldi would show up out of nowhere, verbally abuse me with every curse word known at the time, and then abruptly smack me around a bit. I was too terrified to fight back. And sometimes I ended up with a bonus package of being punched and kicked by all of the gang members as I crawled about the floor picking up my stuff.

It's a tribute to teenage physical resiliency that on occasions when these gorillas pushed me down a flight of steps at school, no bone fractures occurred, just a ton of bruises. Subsequently, the terror followed me onto the public transportation vehicles. Hiraldi and his thugs would slam me against seats and doors and windows. On one occasion they laughingly slashed my coat with switchblade knives. Looking over my shoulder became a way of life. For my first two years of high school, I lived in fear. I hid, I ran, and in the solitude of my own home, I cried!

And then, in 1958, at sixteen years of age, in a time of great hopelessness, fate intervened. One of my diversions from an unpleasant life was basketball. I lived in area schoolyards perfecting my game, and I often traveled at night to the only lighted basketball courts in the area at the Finnegan Playground, some ten blocks from my house.

One evening, on my way home from this ritual hoops practice, I stumbled across my early childhood friend, Sal, badly beaten in an alley behind some row houses. This was not Sal's turf. He was particularly concerned that they were coming back to finish the job on him. He moaned that he was glad to see me. He just knew I would save him! Actually I had little desire to be a hero. And I wasn't really happy to be reunited with Sal under these circumstances. We might not get back to our neighborhood alive. I was in a box with no way out.

As we had grown into our teenage years, Sal and I had drifted apart, partly because I was in the college preparatory track in high school. At that time,

THE BULLY

Sal and Rocco were usually in the suspension track. Eventually, both of my old friends decided to bag high school after their sophomore years. And so we rarely crossed paths. Additionally, Sal was also well established as a teenage gang leader in the neighborhood and was focusing on his business, not school.

In any event, I hadn't even seen Sal in months and suddenly out of the past, there he was lying all bloody on the ground, pleading for me to help him. What choice did I really have? And so I rescued Sal. It wasn't any big deal. I used my body as his crutch and managed to get him home.

Sal's "connected" father kissed me on both cheeks and told me my heroism would never be forgotten. The perps who hurt his son would surely pay for their crime. As for me, the hero, whatever I need, just ask and it would be granted. And so a light went on in my head. I would indeed ask for something.

It was early October. Three weeks had passed since my rescue episode. Sal had fully recovered from his injuries. God only knows what had happened to his attackers, but you can bet it wasn't pretty. In the meantime, I had boldly requested help from the neighborhood version of the Mafia. A plan to deal with Hiraldi was in place. I had been religiously avoiding Hiraldi like the plague he was. But he was about to have his day in court. The setup was in place.

One afternoon after school, I supposedly made the mistake of meandering onto the same trolley car with Hiraldi and his buffoons. They threatened me verbally and shoved me around a bit. More trouble was guaranteed. But this time it wasn't me who was in trouble!

The trolley took us back into our neighborhood. Feinting great fear, I exited the streetcar and quickly disappeared into an abandoned warehouse a few doors away. Hiraldi and his mob followed closely behind. I was making it easy for them. Beating me to a pulp in a secluded place would give them all their macho man orgasms.

Anxious to get their hands on me, Hiraldi and five of his clowns entered the supposedly empty building. What they found instead were Sal and Rocco, the former fondling a sawed-off shotgun and the latter holding a baseball bat. I stood cautiously behind my two protectors.

Fear registered in the eyes of my pursuers. Sal fired a boisterous blast from his shotgun into the roof. Hiraldi's bums dived for the floor. Sal ordered them to stay there face down. All except Hiraldi.

CHAPTER 1

Sal now announced that Hiraldi and I were going to settle our differences permanently. Rocco directed Hiraldi and me into the center of the room. The main event was going to be "Joey vs. Hiraldi!" This was the part of the plan I liked the least! I wasn't sure it would work. Hiraldi smiled and moved toward me with fists cocked; after all, he was used to pummeling me. Of course, what he didn't know was that I had been in training.

Hiraldi swung a wild roundhouse punch at me. I dodged it easily as I had been taught by Rocco and karate kicked Hiraldi squarely in the groin with all the force my right leg could muster. He screamed in pain and covered his crotch with both hands. Too bad, because I next smashed his rodent face with all the might of my best right-hand punch. Pain immediately shot through the knuckles of my hand and raced up my arm. It felt wonderful! Hiraldi imploded. He crumbled to the ground barely conscious and not moving. It was a good thing because I still had a few more Rocco tricks at my disposal!

Sal then made an announcement: Joey was under the protection of his family. To look at me the wrong way would result in the death of the lookee! I thought the message was very clear. But to be sure, Sal and Rocco asked each of Hiraldi's mob to respond to the directive individually. Each of the terrified punks fully agreed to his new contract.

Hiraldi was last. As Sal held him by the hair and Rocco had a knife to his throat, Hiraldi pitifully said that he had never meant me any harm and agreed to never come near me again. The rat pleaded for mercy. I almost felt sorry for him, but not quite.

After about another hour of more rigorous threats from Sal and Rocco, a bruised and bowlegged Hiraldi and his five dunces were released. I tearfully hugged Sal and Rocco and thanked them profusely for everything. I told them that I was tired of school and wanted to be with them in whatever they were doing. Sal told me that that was not going to happen.

"Joey, here's the way it's gonna be," Sal explained. "You've got potential to be something decent, to do something for kids like we were. My father wants you to steer clear of us. You should work at academics and think of being a teacher or maybe even a principal. Schools need good people, and you're good people. It will be best if you just stay away from Rocco and me. As a matter of fact, that's an order from my family: to make something of yourself and then make a difference for them that needs help the most."

Sal and Rocco and I hugged each other again. I felt safe and comfortable and secure with these friends. They had pulled me out of the darkness. But now I was being mandated to go it alone. Luckily, the aura of protection was still there for me. Hiraldi and his cronies never bothered me again. However, this episode colored me for life. As a teacher and school administrator in later years, I was especially vigilant for student bullies and extraordinarily tough on them. Too many educators don't pay enough attention to eliminating bullyism, that despicable practice of student hoodlums who prey on the weak or the different in our schools. No young person should ever have to attend school in an environment of fear.

IT'S ALL ABOUT DREAMS

Living under the protection of the organized crime types is a wonderful thing, especially when you attend an all-boys school in the city. The word was out to stay away from Joey. And basically, the bad guys avoided me during my junior and senior years of high school. I thought that I would now actually be able to focus on things academic. If only life was that simple.

In reality, given my social class background of growing up how and where I did, of being poor and surviving with street smarts rather than book knowledge, too much of what I was being asked to study in school seemed to me to be irrelevant and meaningless. It was hard to care about or concentrate on things like algebra or English literature or chemistry or ancient history, all of which had little to do with my daily survival. For me, most of the high school's curriculum was just gobbledlygook. However, with incredible determination and dreams about becoming something better, I struggled mightily, learned to play the academic game, and finished my college preparatory program in high school with a "B" average. This was no small feat!

The SAT exams that I took in my junior year were especially devastating for me. There was no way that I could handle this bunch of irrelevant nonsense that had nothing to do with my world. And I didn't do well at all. If my SAT scores were an accurate evaluator of my ability, my chances of academic survival in college were not good. I was badly shaken! The good news was that my combined verbal and math score topped 900. The bad

CHAPTER 2

news was that I had a 430 in verbal. My SAT scores foretold my probable demise in college. And becoming a teacher of English was certainly out of the question! Truly, the SAT was the voice of GOD. And it was speaking ominously to me.

Well, the SAT be damned! I wasn't going to give up that easily. I told myself that no stupid test was going to determine my future! I would never submit myself to that humiliating SAT debacle again. Let the cards fall where they fall!

I naively applied to a number of Philadelphia area colleges to which I could commute from my home. Most of them rejected me as unqualified (or was it unfit) to attend their illustrious institutions. Finally, late in the summer following graduation from high school, someone wanted me, or more accurately, said they would admit me. I jumped on the opportunity and entered the Christian Brothers' La Salle College (now La Salle University) in northwest Philly as a daily Broad Street subway commuter in the fall of 1960.

The conventional wisdom among new college students was that freshman composition courses were the most formidable threat for the first year. I had heard plenty of stories about vindictive professors forced by their universities to deliver such courses to the bottom of the academic totem pole, the lowly frosh. These professors took out their wrath on students through arbitrary low grades (A is for God, B is for Professors, C is for Good Student Writers, D is for Adequate Student Writers, and F is for the rest!)

Apprehension as I started college? I was petrified! And with good reason. My SAT had predicted that I had little chance of collegiate success, particularly in the verbal arena. A dreaded English composition course now stared me in the face.

However, by whatever stroke of fate, my first writing course at La Salle was with the legendary and older Brother Clementian, a kindly, knowledgeable, and very effective teacher change-agent who truly shaped my future life.

Brother Clementian was like no other educator I had ever met. To begin, he gave great leeway to his students in choosing theme topics. Incredibly, I was allowed to write about what I knew about. But this Christian Brother was also quite demanding. I had to write for him three times each week. Brother Clementian took great interest in my creative writing about Philadelphia life. This mattered a great deal to my insecure ego! I may not have been Hemingway or Steinbeck, but Brother Clementian read my work with respectful scrutiny. Like all the other students in the class, I received his personal feedback in writing and verbally three times each week. Brother Clementian always offered practical suggestions to improve my different pieces of writing. And there was always a required rewrite.

Most important, Brother Clementian kept telling me that I could someday be a good writer if I worked at it and that I had potential. Finally, this saintly college professor utilized a motivational grading scale whereby a 10.0 was the highest possible grade. Every theme I authored for Brother Clementian received between a 9.0 and 10.0 numerical value to accompany his commentary. My writing was hardly that good. But this wily Christian Brother had no intention of devastating his insecure and budding writers with low grades. Brother Clementian was the master of positive reinforcement. Grades were used to build rather than to bludgeon. He made me want to write with his patience and shrewdness and love. And I got much better at it!

All of this was very different from what I eventually heard from fellow students about so many negative freshman composition course experiences at La Salle as well as at other universities. Being in one of those classrooms would likely have ended my college career forever.

Instead, I had somehow fallen into the lap of Brother Clementian. Aside from Rocco and Sal and the mob, now someone from the foreign land of academia had expressed some faith in me. More than anything else, Brother Clementian's constant encouragement gave me confidence that just maybe the SAT was not infallible and that I could compete with the more privileged. After one semester with this magician Christian Brother, I now had hope that I might be able to get through La Salle and become an English teacher. And Brother Clementian's daily educational practice with all of his students shaped my educational philosophy, which to this day remains unchanged.

Mediocre teachers are validators. They take students as they come to them, label them, quantify them, and endorse their background/baggage with an appropriate grade that defines the pupil's worth. In contrast, great teachers are somehow able to effect positive change in all students who come to them, no matter what problems or lack of skills they bring with them. Great teachers foster growth and inspire self-confidence in the students who have been written off, the ones no one else wants. Great teachers don't squash dreams, they build them!

REFLECTIONS ON MY WORK IN CAMDEN CITY

Amazingly enough, I was graduated from La Salle University as a properly certified Teacher of English in June of 1964. I was filled with idealism and ready to save the world. But no school district wanted me. Getting a job was much tougher that I could have imagined. I had flooded suburban Pennsylvania's school systems with applications and ended up with only one unsuccessful interview in three months. By late August, I was desperate and despondent. And so just a few days before schools were scheduled to open, I crossed the bridge into New Jersey and visited downtown Camden City Hall, where this fearsome urban school district's headquarters were located.

I filled out an application and interviewed with an Italian American assistant superintendent, Dr. Frank. Unbelievably, one of Camden's English teachers had resigned that very morning. I bragged about my practice teaching experience in Philadelphia's inner city the previous spring. It was all that I had to sell myself. Then the conversation switched to Italian neighborhoods and growing up in Philly. Dr. Frank liked the idea of former city kids teaching city kids. He took me in to meet the Italian American superintendent, Dr. Anthony.

"Nails," Dr. Frank addressed Dr. Anthony. "I got this paisan here. This boy looks good. He knows city kids. Matter of fact, he is one. I'm gonna hire him." I stood in stunned silence. After two months of frustration with more than twenty-five school districts that wouldn't even interview me, I had my first job in the wink of an eye. Indeed, that was exactly what Dr. Anthony did. He winked at me. I cautiously winked back!

CHAPTER 3

In my first teaching assignment with seventh and eighth graders housed in an elementary school, I had a female ex-military officer as principal. Mrs. Irene was rigid and by the book and put the fear of God in me. None of this was bad for someone starting out.

About one month into my teaching experience at Camden, I stopped by the school office very late in the afternoon. I found Mrs. Irene, my tough principal, sobbing in her office. I walked in without being invited and sat down. For awhile there was awkward silence. And then Mrs. Irene told me everything.

She had reached the end of her rope with a bunch of post-high school age thugs who took over the school grounds every night and drank and smashed bottles onto the playgrounds. They regularly vandalized the school with graffiti and broke windows whenever the booze so inspired them. Mrs. Irene had contacted the cops, but policing school grounds was hardly the top priority in Camden. And the police claimed that whenever a random squad car was sent to the school, the grounds were deserted.

Last night, Mrs. Irene had confronted the hoodlums late in the evening. This woman had courage. She had been polite and asked them to think about not ruining the school experience for little kids. The punks responded with curses and threats and chased her away!

Mrs. Irene's description of the event was ugly. She was embarrassed and without any hope. She thanked me for listening. I headed home without responding. I wanted to help but wasn't sure how to do it. The answer came to me while driving home. Later that evening, I telephoned Sal. I requested a small favor.

Three days later, my eighth-grade morning homeroom was abuzz with tales of Mafia gangsters in the school yard on the previous night. I was dying of curiosity. I probed the kids for information. Here's what I was able to piece together. Apparently, six guys in suits and ties and sunglasses had shown up in a shiny black limousine—sort of the Blues Brothers visit Camden! The well-dressed visitors had gone over to the more than twenty schoolyard hoods and talked to them. Well, actually, the six guys in the suits gave the thugs some emphatic marching orders.

Some of the neighborhood eyewitnesses who watched from surrounding homes claimed the limousine six all had guns drawn. Well, whatever it takes to drive home a message. Just a bit of animated talking according to most witnesses. After which the nocturnal rats who inhabited the playground walked off the school grounds. This was very wise on their part! Judgment had been rendered. The street toughs had been banned forever from the school property by a higher authority. Obviously, they accepted the verdict. Fear can be a great motivator in life. And these vagrants must have found a new rat hole because they never returned for their nightly habitation of the schoolyard. Mrs. Irene had to wonder about all of this, but I don't think she ever connected the dots as to how this miracle had occurred. Score one for the Wise Guys, subtle and very effective.

The night after the showdown in Camden, I telephoned Sal and thanked him profusely. I told him that out of gratitude I would treat Rocco and him to a dinner at our favorite restaurant, Palumbo's Nostalgia Room in South Philadelphia. Sal declined, politely but firmly reiterating once again that I was to keep way from Rocco and him. He reminded me that I was supposed to become the best teacher I could be. That would be thanks enough!

In my first Camden teaching assignment, Merritt was the science teacher in the classroom adjacent to mine. He was a superb mentor. Merritt taught me a wealth of psychology and technique about motivating and handling urban kids. We became good friends, the first time I ever had a close black friend in my life. We had great times together. His hyena laugh was infectious and made me laugh so hard that I cried. I too learned to laugh like a hyena.

Merritt introduced me to some Camden bars. Many times I was the only white person present. Merritt and I drank many martinis together and philosophized about the world of teaching.

About a year after I first met Merritt, I dragged him to the wedding of one of our female colleagues in Scranton, Pennsylvania. Merritt didn't want to go, but I was persistent. First off, a black and a white guy eating meals together in area restaurants and then sharing a motel room in 1964 turned more than a few Scranton heads. But that was nothing compared with the wedding reception that was held in a very exclusive country club whose claim to fame was that it did not admit Jews. Now they were going to have a black guy invading their whiteness.

Merritt was certain that the country club staff would be dressed in Klu Klux Klan sheets. I kept telling him that we were a lot tougher that these Scranton hicks. The Klan had better not mess with us. We were from Camden! So we just stormed right into the wedding. To our surprise, everyone

CHAPTER 3

was very polite, but I sensed the spotlight that Merritt was in because of being the only African American in the room. It was a real world lesson of the times. I didn't like it very much. I know that Merritt was glad to finally get back to Camden. Incredibly enough, so was I. Country clubs and rich white people were just not my thing. I missed being with my Camden kids. It was where I belonged.

People are always amazed when I tell them that teaching in inner-city Camden was a joyful experience. My students were energetic bundles, bright and sassy and fun. I set limits and drew lines for behavior and never had a problem. We got on famously. Maybe it was our common roots. But I liked these real kids, and they knew it. They soon grew to like me.

So I worked them like dogs using the Brother Clementian model of positive reinforcement. I demanded two written assignments per week from each of my 120 pupils. The students started much of this writing in class as I meandered around their desks. It was my clever plan to make sure that assignments would get finished. And they almost always did.

At home, I spent on average fifteen hours per week, tirelessly reading every paper, sprinkling each with constructive suggestions and adding a generous grade. I was determined to make a difference in their lives. Rewrites were a requirement, and after a few months my classroom walls were jammed with student masterpieces on display. My students and I got into a rut, a wonderful, academic pathway, and most of my Camden kids learned to write and do it pretty well. I have no idea what happened at other schools, but district supervisors were constantly visiting my classes and taking notes on what I was doing.

In the summer of 1965, with federal money pouring into education, I was offered a three-month job with Operation Head Start. I had no idea what that was but I needed money and accepted the post. I soon found that I would be teaching twenty preschoolers from the heart of North Camden's ghetto. Terror overwhelmed me. What was I going to do?

From growing up in Philadelphia, I thought I knew what it was to be poor. Clothes with stitched-up tears and holes in them were ordinary to me. I often put cardboard inside my shoes when the soles wore through. Nobody I knew ever had any money. And then there was food.

I remember being invited over for dinner to a ten-year-old friend's house across the street from our row house. I had never done anything like this before. My mother surprisingly gave me the required permission and was I ever excited.

Georgie had eight brothers and sisters. We all gathered around a scratched and chipped uncovered table in the tiny dining room. No parents were seated with us. Georgie's mom appeared and tossed three loaves of white bread and some butter knives onto the table. She then added two bottles of catsup, one oversized jar of mayonnaise, and a five-pound bag of sugar. Let the feast begin!

The kids all dived in grabbing pieces of bread and creating one of the specials of the night, either a catsup, mayonnaise, or sugar sandwich. I followed suit opting for the mayo. Most of us ate three sandwiches, including me. We also had soda to drink. The good news was that no one left the table hungry. The bad news was that this sure wasn't my mom's spaghetti, fried chicken wings, or homemade meatloaf. Compared with this family, mine ate like kings.

And then along came North Camden, a third world of the most impoverished humans I had ever seen. It was really hard to believe this was the United States. Most of the Head Start children I met lived in poverty and squalor light years below the working-class neighborhood in which I was raised.

So there I was, challenged to get these deprived Lilliputians off to a good educational start. And me with no experience or ideas on how to do it. We had an orientation day with the kids and their parents (mostly moms). Out of desperation, I hooked up with a colleague and we took our children and their parents on a field trip to the nearby Delaware River. The children were excited by the experience of seeing bridges and large ships but especially in talking with some old fishermen who were actually reeling in catfish, striped bass, and shad from the banks of the river. Suddenly, I had a gem of an idea.

When we returned to school I seated the parents in the rear of the classroom and assured them very briefly that I was going to do my best for their children. I then read the kids a scintillating story from my classroom library about Willie the Fish. If Sal and Rocco could only see me now!

The book sparked a one-hour discussion about rivers, fishes, and other related wonders. The little kids just bubbled! Children and parents seemed to be satisfied with their new instructor. I had survived my first half-day session, and I now had a survival plan. It was Friday and I wouldn't see the

CHAPTER 3

children again until the following Wednesday when Head Start started for real. I had plenty of time to get ready.

After work, I made a visit to a local restaurant supply business in Camden. Sal and Rocco had recommended the place. I was seeking a bargain for the purchase of some stuff for my Head Start classroom. I told the Wise Guy supply store owners that I was a starving Camden teacher. They were very curious about what I wanted to order, especially when I told them it was going to be used for the education of poor kids from their own city. We gabbed a bit about growing up in Italian neighborhoods. The Wise Guys offered to donate the works. I readily accepted. I probably could have been a great used car salesman if I wasn't a teacher.

Monday and Tuesday were "get ready" days for teachers. Most were hanging colorful decorations and posters. However, at 9:00 A.M. on Monday morning, everyone's attention was focused outside. A huge delivery truck had showed up at the Cooper Poynt School. It looked like a Mafia tank. The driver and his partner, two huge bulls, unloaded the contents of the truck into my classroom. Teachers watched in amazement.

And so I began my creation. Student chairs and tables were moved to the sidelines of my classroom. A trio of eight-foot-by-six-foot restaurant wall mirrors were placed face up carefully side by side in the center of the floor. This would be our lake. Sand was then placed in a one foot width all around the perimeter of the mirror (lake) to create a shoreline. Artificial plants and flowers in various baskets and containers that came in the truck delivery were then placed atop the sand at the shoreline of the lake. Finally, huge stones and rocks were used to add even more realism to the lake shore.

The delivery also included more than twenty broom handles without the brooms on the end. These would be our fishing rods. I attached about three foot of string (fishing line) to each pole. At the end of the fishing line I affixed one of the magnets from my supply order. Meanwhile, my adult classroom helper who was convinced I was bonkers was busy drawing facsimiles of different kinds of fish from the encyclopedia. They ranged from six inches to one yard in length. Together we colored them appropriately with crayons and cut them out with scissors. The fishes, with paper clips on their mouths so that they could *bite* the magnet hooks, were then placed randomly onto the mirror. Anglers would have a field day! The last step for me was to gather up every book that I could find in our school about fish, boats, lakes, and rivers. I located more than twenty. All was in readiness.

To make this long story short, I became famous in 1965 as one of America's most clever Head Start teachers, a master of early childhood interdisciplinary units. The feds even made some sort of documentary film about what a superb job I was doing with my Head Starters. In fact, I was just a desperate teacher who created an imaginary lake full of fish in the middle of his classroom. Over that incredible summer, fish inspired every imaginable kind of preschool learning: creative and analytical thinking, spelling and lettering, studies of species, sizes, coloring, shapes, measurements, exercises, costume parties, and even basic angler skills via some guest lectures from local experts who fished the Delaware River.

The Camden experience for me was one of the most exhilarating of my life. I coached junior high basketball, chased my kids off corners at night, took small groups of kids on a myriad of authorized and unauthorized educational field trips, and chaperoned a hundred different school events. Being a teacher is so much more than just directing the learning activities in a classroom. It's also being a surrogate parent, a counselor, and a missionary.

It was challenging, formidable, and exhausting. I was changing the world one kid at a time and loving every minute of it. And contrary to the prediction of the SAT, I had even managed to earn a master's degree in my spare time. Predictably, after six years of this freneticism, I was also very tired.

In 1970, La Salle College gave me the chance to return to campus as the director of sports information. I needed a change mentally and physically. And this was too good an opportunity to pass up. Besides I was depressed. Sal and Rocco had been convicted of something and were sent to jail.

Getting paid to work in sports? You've got to be kidding! I reluctantly left the Camden Public School System in 1970, wondering if I had sold out on everything in which I believed.

MY LIFE IN ACADEMIA

Going back to my undergraduate alma mater as a college administrator was an awesome prospect. The job required top-notch writing skills, creativity, and the ability to work on deadlines. La Salle was giving me a marvelous opportunity, believing in me once again. I was determined to give it my best shot.

My new boss was Bob, a very savvy public relations guy who had directed the La Salle news bureau for many years. Bob was the editor of the quarterly alumni magazine, interacted daily with college and faculty leaders, and generated most of the major news releases on college happenings. He also worked at enticing feature stories from the major Philadelphia news media, and he developed promotional films and slide shows.

My assignments included editing a monthly newsletter full of academic papers from faculty members (who, me?) and generating publicity for La Salle's acclaimed summer music theater. I also did promotional work for the entire sports program. But my primary responsibility was maximizing the publicity for La Salle's one big-time NCAA sport, basketball. Like many institutions around America, winning seasons in Division 1 football or basketball translate into tons of free publicity and name recognition for universities. In point of fact, if you ask people around the United States to recite any fact they might know about La Salle, many can tell you that the great Tom Gola led the college to both the NCAA and the NIT championships in the early 1950s. Through the 1960s and the 1970s, the Big Five basketball rivalries

CHAPTER 4

between Villanova, Temple, Pennsylvania, St. Joseph's, and La Salle at the University of Pennsylvania Palestra offered the best sports attraction in Philadelphia and one of the best in the country. These Philly colleges got plenty of newspaper coverage. And in 1970, when I took over La Salle's sports information position, I walked right into the middle of that heated excitement.

The worst part of the sports information job was plane travel in the blustery air turbulence of winter. La Salle played in arenas from coast to coast, and I accompanied them to help promote our games in the local press wherever we played. We often landed on snowy runways or had the plane de-iced just before takeoff. On many of those flights, I piously made promises to God about doing good works if I would just get home safely. I ended up in heavy debt to the Lord.

Chicago and Buffalo in January were two of my least favorite places. That's because it was always snowing in both of these cities. The North Pole has nothing on either of these refrigerators. On most occasions, La Salle's traveling party included a doctor and a priest. I was grateful because I figured that if I was going to get physically damaged or die in some plane crash, I was well covered.

The most difficult part of sports information was the game night deadlines. Often, the Philadelphia newspapers opted to not send a reporter with us. In such cases, I was required to feed the game coverage back to the *Philadelphia Bulletin* and the *Philadelphia Inquirer*. For La Salle games out west in different time zones this presented tight timelines. On Saturday nights in particular both papers had prescribed deadlines around midnight (EST), and they weren't about to hold the presses for a story of La Salle's latest basketball game.

For a sports information director there could be no more important task than just making sure the game story hit the next day's papers. I was forced to write rapid fire. Almost no time to be creative or rewrite. Just get it done. Say something clever that summarized the game, lay out some thorough and accurate facts, and fire the story back to the newspaper at ninety miles an hour. Talk about learning by doing. Talk about no room for error. Talk about white heat pressure!

The most intriguing aspect of sports information experience at La Salle was with the head basketball coach, Paul. We arrived together in 1970.

Coach Paul struck me as being caught in some time warp. To me, he was really some kind of Arthurian knight in search of the Holy Grail who was gobbled up by a time machine and thrust into the role of a college basketball coach.

Coach Paul was very Catholic. Mass and Holy Communion were required game/battle preparations. Nothing could be more important to basketball wars than a pure heart. Indeed, I remember having to rent a car somewhere in the Bible Belt so that I could drive the coach sixty miles to a lonely Catholic Church for Mass on game day. It didn't take La Salle's athletic department too long to figure out that it would be a lot more economical to just send a priest on road trips with the team. And so Father Ray, a delightful Dominican, became a fixture in our traveling party. He said Mass prior to every game in one of our motel rooms. Father Ray prepared us all as knights in armor going into basketball battles. It was all pretty cool!

The physician who traveled with the team was Dr. Gene, a well-respected humanitarian with a great sense of humor. He loved the La Salle players and cared for them like they were his children. The doc and I spent much time together sipping martinis around the United States, and he became a father figure to me as well. Several years later, I agonizingly wrote his obituary on deadline after the doc suffered a fatal coronary attack on the La Salle bench in the middle of a game. I still miss him to this day.

Coach Paul's first season at La Salle was a terrific one. Led by Ken, a superb player, the team had national ranking for most of the year. I did a lot of inexpensive but effective promotional work for Ken, and he attained All-America status. But that achievement was much more because of Ken's outstanding point and rebounding totals than because of me. Nevertheless, a major American newspaper called my promotional work "the cleverest in America."

The following year, with most of our best players having been graduated, Coach Paul had to build the team around the lone returning player, Jim, a smallish six-foot, three-inch forward. The coach challenged me to create some excitement for the coming year. No problem. I was an evolving public relations wizard.

I posed Jim for pictures in uniform on top of a three-foot-high table next to the basket hoop. Because he was on the table, his elbows were well above the rim. For more realism, I had him slam-dunk the ball by jumping off the

CHAPTER 4

table a few times while we snapped pictures. With the bottoms of the photographs neatly cropped, Jim now looked like the greatest leaper the world had ever seen. In fact, Jim could jump pretty well and easily dunk the ball, but when I was done with him, he looked like a human flying machine.

Jim was dubbed "The Skyman" in our publicity materials, and I featured his flying act on the cover. In spite of a mediocre campaign in terms of wins and losses, La Salle got lots of national attention for this remarkable player who could soar above the other players. Jim had a great season as an individual player. As we traveled America, newspaper after newspaper previewed our games with invitations to the local populace to come out and see La Salle's "Skyman." I too was flying high! I was damn good at what I was doing.

One thing about the public relations business, though. No one cares about yesterday. Only what will you do tomorrow. And Coach Paul was soon at it again with a new project for me. During the summer of 1972, he had coached athletes in Brazil on some sort of goodwill mission from our government. When he returned, I interviewed him and created a nice story about his Brazilian experiences that gained some national exposure for the coach. But that wasn't enough. Coach Paul showed me some statuettes he had brought back from Brazil. Basically, these featured a closed right hand with the thumb protruding through the second and third fingers. I had no idea what any of this was about.

Coach Paul then informed me that these images from Brazil should be the basis of my promotional campaign for the 1972-73 La Salle basketball season. I could splatter this Brazilian symbol throughout our brochures and even have it made into cloth logos that could be sewed onto the team uniforms. Just what I needed: a basketball coach as my public relations assistant!

All of this was too easy. Something just didn't feel right. I decided to do some research. I located some Brazilian nationals through the Philadelphia International House. They explained to me that the item in question was macumba. And what they told me next scared me to death: "To many, the macumba is a kind of black magic. It is not to be trivialized. Bad fortune to any and all of those who make light of it!"

One thing I'm not is stupid! I crossed off Coach Paul's Brazilian promotional plan on the spot. Predictably, when I told the coach about it later that afternoon, he was miffed. I had better come up with something just as glitzy or else. Sure, Coach Paul, and how about something that doesn't get us all killed by voodoo black magic?

For several weeks, my mind raced in search of some unique idea to promote La Salle basketball for the 1972-73 season. And then one morning I passed the coach on campus as he walked to the English class he was teaching that semester. Coach Paul had a master's degree in English literature with some concentrated study of William Shakespeare. The light went on in my perverse brain. Always look for opportunity in the midst of adversity. What an idea! Coach Paul as the only college basketball mentor in America who was a Shakespearean scholar.

I raced over to the college library and checked out a Shakespearean thesaurus. It was all over but the research and some hard work. And so it came to pass that I created the La Salle basketball preview for 1972-73 utilizing an interview with Coach Paul that existed only in my imagination. And it was truly a work of art:

- About improving over last year's losing season: "Woe to the hand that shed that costly blood." (*Julius Caesar*)
- About being optimistic after a losing season: "Wise men never sit and wail their loss, but cheerily seek how to redress their harms." (*Henry IV*)
- About new coaching strategies for the coming year: "O mischief, thou art swift to enter in the thoughts of desperate men." (*Romeo and Juliet*)
- About this year's team spirit: "Would to God you were of our determination." (*Henry IV*)
- About having several veteran players return this year: "I shall have so much experience for my pains." (*Othello*)
- About three returnees who started last year: "Three proper young men of excellent growth and presence." (*As You Like It*)
- About our one best player returning this year: "He makes sweet music." (*Two Gentlemen of Verona*)
- About our top incoming sophomore player: "Yond Cassius has a lean and hungry look." (*Julius Caesar*)
- About the potential of our other new players this year: "Wondrous qualities." (*The Taming of the Shrew*)

CHAPTER 4

- About a prediction for the coming season: "To climb steep hills requires slow pace at first." (*Henry VIII*); and, "Be patient; tomorrow 't shall be mended." (*The Taming of the Shrew*)
- About many good teams on the schedule: "They that stand high have many blasts to shake them; And if they fall, they dash themselves to pieces." (*Richard III*)
- About any surprises for opponents: "Have more than thou showest, Speak less than thou knowest." (*King Lear*)
- And to sum it all up: "It is not madness That I have uttered; Bring me to the test." (*Hamlet*)

Well, you have to admit it. This college basketball preview was certainly different, a unique masterpiece. And that's exactly how several national newspapers and television networks evaluated it. La Salle's name got some national play. Coach Paul was forever cemented as a celebrity bard accomplice of Shakespeare in the Philadelphia media and across America. And, yes, he is the same guy who a couple of years later coached the Los Angeles Lakers to an NBA championship. I know for sure because I subsequently watched a television sports special on CBS about the NBA's Coach Paul, the Shakespearean leader of Magic Johnson and the rest of the Lakers.

My years at La Salle were truly wonderful ones. Great colleagues, eager, bright student workers all around, and a very friendly environment in which to work. I probably could have lived happily ever after at the college. But after five years, something began to gnaw at my insides. Sports publicity was great fun. It was also frivolous. I needed to get back to a job where I could make meaningful change in the world. Silly me. I had this thing about not wanting to go through a life without significance. And besides that, in my fearful moments of air travel with La Salle's basketball teams, I had made promises to a higher authority. Working in sports publicity would never repay the debt I owed!

5

COMMUNITY TURMOIL

In January of 1975, I saw a classified advertisement in one of the Philadelphia newspapers for a communications director in the Upper Darby School District, a suburban school system just west of Philadelphia (PA). Going back to public education was something I wanted to do. The idea of doing so as an administrator added to the appeal. Two months later, I left my dream job at La Salle and started my new career in school public relations. It was a brand new position for the Upper Darby School District. I was very excited about being able to initiate an unprecedented communications program in the public sector. From my La Salle experience, I was now armed with well-honed writing and creative thinking skills. I couldn't wait to get started.

Having read some materials from the National School Public Relations Association prior to my arrival at the new job in Upper Darby, I was filled with idealistic ideas of building two-way communication channels between the school board and its administration with parents of students and the community at large as well as with staff and the news media. I would be the catalyst in creating an informed, caring constituency that would better understand the role, needs, goals, and accomplishments of the school district. What a terrific use of my public relations skills. What a fantasy!

All of this was a wee bit too idealistic. The real world hardly ever works that way. Contrary to my aspirations, I was hired for an agenda that was hardly my own. First, the school district had experienced an ugly teacher

CHAPTER 5

union strike in 1974. The school board felt that they got the worst of it in the public debate that surrounded the work stoppage. And so when the next teachers' strike would come in a couple of years (how's that for optimism and a spirit of compromise), the new public relations director would swing the tide of public opinion to the management side.

The second purpose of hiring me had to do with impending school closings. The Upper Darby School District's pupil enrollment had declined from its all-time high of just under 13,000 students to fewer than 8,000 pupils. Neighborhood schools were about to be closed, and, in theory, a public relations practitioner could simply smooth over the community turmoil that would occur. Dream on!

And, finally, the school board in their infinite wisdom had determined that it was time for the local press to be brought under control. As if this were in the realm of human possibility—talk about an aura of doom. I really had no chance to succeed.

Added to all of this, my new working conditions left much to be desired. I wondered about how much belief the school system really had in this new position. The school district did not provide me with a secretary and isolated me in a former closet with a typewriter as my only friend. I soon found out that I was the lowest paid administrator in the entire system. Why would anyone take me seriously?

Access to the top-level administration was tightly controlled by empowered secretaries. Getting to see a colleague down the hall could only be accomplished by appointment, and sometimes it took many hours if not a day. A visit with the superintendent could sometimes be as difficult to arrange as getting an audience with the pope. And many administrators, especially the fifteen school principals, naively viewed public relations as something dirty at worst and unnecessary at best.

The school board held evening public meetings twice monthly. These were bland affairs in which official business was formally adopted and a few citizens would publicly berate the school directors on the issue of the month. On each occasion, the school board would then adjourn into closed sessions that lasted well past midnight. Board members would pontificate and fight over individual agendas with each other. Only the superintendent was permitted to take part in these debates and discussions. The rest of the administrators sat on their hands and watched. And of course no one asked lowly me anything. Further, the idea of me volunteering any ideas was anathema.

It gets worse. On every Friday afternoon, there was a central administration staff meeting beginning at 1:00 P.M. and lasting until as late as 5:00 P.M. Conducted by the superintendent of schools, these were weekly opportunities for each top-level administrator to prove to the boss that he or she had been working all week. In theory, I suppose these sessions were for group problem solving. But in my view, these military model meetings were the most useless "show and tell" time wasters in the history of mankind. What a great way to end a week. I would get back to my tiny office with my blood pressure boiling over and find twenty telephone messages lying next to piles of work I hadn't been able to touch because I had been sitting in these stupid staff meetings.

After just a few weeks in the Upper Darby School District, I truly hated the place. It was rigid and stuffy and depressing. I wanted to leave, but there was no place to go. I knew I was doomed to disaster.

Well, wait just a minute here, Bozo! Aren't you the one that took this new job without asking the right questions? Truly, there was really no one to blame but myself. Better that I just get busy! I immersed myself in the tasks that I thought were important.

I was allowed to establish a citizens' committee of public affairs. We conducted a random sample community survey, gathered objective feedback, and established goals for the school public relations program. Several pragmatic curriculum and instruction forums for the general public emerged from this survey.

On another front, it was essential that I change the internal mindset of Upper Darby's educators about public relations. I badgered the school principals in their monthly meetings about the need for meaningful ongoing communication with their constituencies: "School public relations is hardly something dirty. It's telling your public what your doing in the schools and why. It's also doing a good job and then publicizing it. And it's a critical necessity in the business of public education."

This was a very slow process. But eventually most of the principals began to work with me in generating press releases about educational stuff that mattered. At my suggestion, some of the principals even began hosting periodic breakfast or luncheon meetings for educational discussions with groups of

CHAPTER 5

parents. Others set up parental visits to classrooms when schools were in session. These were major breakthroughs.

With the advice and counsel of my new citizens' committee, I designed and produced a substantive monthly newsletter focused on teaching and learning and circulated it to more than 30,000 residents. It got rave reviews and won awards. And finally I overhauled and improved an internal informational monthly newsletter to better communicate with our 1,000 staff members. However, I was really fiddling away while Rome was burning. That's because none of this even came close to blowing away the dark clouds on the horizon.

The teacher strike of 1977 was guaranteed. A predetermined holocaust. Still tasting the bitter remnants of the last work stoppage debacle three years earlier, each side had little use for compromise and vowed to crush each other. I became the voice of John the Baptist crying out in the school system wilderness with no one listening. And the schools and the community were about to suffer once again.

In the public spotlight surrounding the multiweek strike, I did some of my best work ever. But I'm not proud of it at all. The rhetoric of the public statements that I created for the board leadership had a sharp sting. And I designed several newspaper ads that were things of ugly beauty.

Board members, administrators, teachers, students, parents, and community members fought with one another in a situation spinning absurdly out of control. When the strike was all over, one quarter of one point in salary increases was all that had separated the two sides.

A state arbitrator finally settled a new contract. Teachers and management claimed victory. In reality, everyone lost. And just an ounce of compromise by each side could have avoided what it would now take years to heal.

As bad as all of this was, there was little time to take a few deep breaths. For now, in the aftermath of all of this labor-management hostility, the issue of school closings loomed on the horizon. So the community's burning. So what. Let's start a few more fires.

Under intense pressure from taxpayer groups, the school board closed one of its junior high schools in 1977, ripping the heart out of the Clifton Heights (PA) community where the school was located. And now three or four elementary schools, traditional fixtures in their Upper Darby neighborhoods, were also on the chopping block!

COMMUNITY TURMOIL

In one of those horrible late night closed meetings of the school board, the superintendent of schools was called onto the carpet for his alleged avoidance of the school closings issue. The school board wanted action. The Upper Darby School District needed to save more money. Board members chastised the super for inaction. Talk is always cheap in the middle of the night. And I don't think that the school board ever figured that their superintendent, a former Marine colonel, would dare to give them exactly what they had mandated.

I violated administrative rules and spoke out. I begged the school board and the superintendent to slow down: "We had better prepare the community for this!" No one was listening. We were racing toward the edge of a cliff for no sane reason.

One week later, the superintendent publicly unveiled a plan to close four neighborhood elementary schools. It was like an atomic bomb. Politicians, clergy, civic organizations, student, parent, and teacher constituencies, and the local press rose up in unison against this plan that had come down from the mountain out of nowhere. This was a classic how not to do it. Predictably, within a few days, more than 2,000 people jammed the senior high auditorium to rail against the school closing plan.

Ironically, the superintendent who had only done what he was ordered to do by the school board took all the heat. Only when he now looked behind him, no one was there. The majority of the school board had jumped ship. They were just innocent elected official bystanders. This was now the superintendent's unilateral plan for school closings!

Two interesting things then happened. First, a major private sector corporation offered me more money than I ever dreamt about to become their vice president of public relations; so I resigned from the Upper Darby School District. And second, just a couple of weeks before I was scheduled to exit the Upper Darby School District forever, the superintendent had a heart attack. Within days, an angry superintendent of schools fired off a public letter from his recovery bed telling the school board which had repudiated him to essentially "find themselves a new superintendent" and buy out his contract. The board readily cut a deal—the superintendent was out. Several top level administrators simultaneously announced retirements and departures for greener pastures. The school district was in shambles. I couldn't wait to get out!

6

BACK INTO THE FRAY

It was the weekend before I was to start my new executive vice president job in the private sector. I had packed my belongings and departed the school district forever on the previous Friday. The Sunday morning telephone call came from Mike, the Upper Darby School District's business manager and one of the few remaining central administrators still around from the now defunct central administration regime. I had only been gone twenty-four hours, but a great deal was happening behind the scenes in the school system.

Mike was a very complex figure. I always felt he was much more human than the rest of the cast of central administrators with whom I worked. He was a fierce watchdog of school district money, a powerful manager of people, a very shrewd politician, and an avid student of people dynamics. He was a good listener endowed with a great sense of humor. And he could curse with the best of sailors. His persona was controlled by internal switches. He could go from being terrifying to intellectual to warm and fuzzy depending on the situation. And now on the telephone, he switched on his best country bumpkin disguise. I was being seduced by a master of the art.

Mike never wasted words: Golly gee, things had changed! And I was needed back in the school district more than ever! Mike told me that the school board was about to elect him as the new superintendent of schools. A bunch of administrative people were leaving. He pleaded with me to remain with the district. He said my talents had previously been underutilized and

CHAPTER 6

wasted. Mike planned to make me his chief confidant. He had always admired my brainpower. I would eventually be elevated to an assistant superintendent position, a commissioned officer for the school system. Say what? Who, me? My new duties would combine the public relations function with personnel duties for the system. I nearly fainted hearing all of this.

"What are those private sector thieves going to pay you?" Mike inquired. "We'll match the salary offer whatever it is. I need you back here. I'll give you the chance to do great things. Talk to that pretty wife of yours and call me back today. You'll never be sorry."

So I'm a wee bit impulsive! My wife, Joan, just shook her head in disbelief. She immediately knew which way I was leaning. But was it over a mountain side? Joan and I were doing something that we had never done before, drinking martinis at 11:30 A.M.! I called Mike back in fifteen minutes. I told him that the corporation hiring me planned to pay me $25,000 per annum. I had previously been making $16,000 per year in the school system. Mike told me that matching the private sector salary number would be no problem. I reneged on my resignation from the school district on the spot. Mike bubbled gleefully with gratitude over the phone. What in heaven's name had I just done?

On Monday, I arrived at my alleged new private sector job. I immediately informed the astounded president of the corporation welcoming my arrival that my train had been derailed. I was staying in the Upper Darby School District. It became very obvious to me that no one had ever done what I was doing in the presence of this regal CEO. The guy just stared at me in amazement. His eyes were bulging out of his head. He quietly asked me if I was out of my mind. I told him that I probably was. My knees were shaking badly. I quickly exited corporate America and went back to the Upper Darby School District.

Confused fellow workers in the Upper Darby Administration Building just glared at me in stunned silence as I carried all my books and personal belongings back into the closet office I had vacated the previous Friday. April fool... Joey's back! That same evening, the school board made it all official. Not only was my resignation rescinded but I was promoted. So you like to ride on roller coasters? Just stick with me. I'll show you how it's done.

True to his promise, Mike and I started every morning with brainstorming strategy sessions over coffee. Our chief priority was initially the school closing mess. Mike asked me for my advice. Now that was incredibly refreshing. In response to the public outcry, we agreed upon a one-year moratorium on any school closings to let things cool off. Since trust in the school district had all but been destroyed, I suggested that we hire external consultants to validate the need for school closings and determine which schools should be closed. The consultants would be required to utilize community input in arriving at their conclusions, preferably via a broad-based committee representing every constituency in the school district. Open communication with the news media throughout this process would be our mandate. And finally I stressed that the explanation of the eventual school closing plan should be the responsibility of the consultants. In my view, they were getting paid not just to develop the plan but to defend it as well.

Mike and I talked about all of this in detail. We finalized the strategy. No decisions would be made for one year. The matter of potential school closings would be thoroughly studied by our independent consultants in full view of the public. As things evolved, Mike and I would focus on regularly communicating with all the key players—school board members and teacher, administrator, parent, political, and community leaders. We would use a variety of forums. And finally, we charged the consultants with making sure that there would be a consistent and up-to-date public information flow to the news media, all employees, and the community at large.

This process involved a ton of difficult communication work. And it was worth it. Suffice to say, that one year later three elementary schools in the Upper Darby School District were closed because of declining enrollments. And this was accomplished without very much community protest and strife. It's not *what* you do in public sector management, it's *how* you do it that really makes the difference!

It's ironic that Mike's primary background was on the business side. He did not come to the top from the usual educational practitioner background of the principalship or instructional/curricular administration. He did not even possess the usual overrated doctorate in education. And yet the primary changes effected during his superintendency involved significant educational improvements. Maybe that's because Mike never considered himself to be omniscient. He engaged in lots of "bottom-up" thinking, listening carefully to people in the trenches. Mike spent lots of time in bars with school district, community, and other elected leaders where he practiced

CHAPTER 6

his marvelous skills as a political manipulator. He bounced a million ideas off other people, including me. He was always processing, contriving, revising, and planning.

During his tenure, curriculum articulation of subject matter between grade levels throughout the school system was dramatically improved. Academic prerequisites for high school graduation were enhanced in all major curriculum areas. Line and staff relationships between all school district administrators were clarified and enforced. Relationships with the teachers' union were never better. After two successive strikes, a new contract was waltzed into place. And a new teacher appraisal system that stressed productive teaching without being threatening to the professional staff was put into place. In summary, Mike was a very effective superintendent of schools. More important for me, he was the greatest of teachers.

PERSONNEL ADVENTURES

Having the personnel arena added to my public relations administrative duties in the school district was essentially the way that Superintendent Mike was able to get two things for me: advancement and more money. It also gave me migraine headaches.

I didn't exactly come to the personnel management function with great preparation. Nothing in my graduate training at the University of Pennsylvania prepared me for the massive amount of contradictory detail, inconsistency, and chaos that existed regarding the record of human dealings with more than 1,000 employees as well as the maze of contractual and policy dealings with three different unions. It was all overwhelming—a mind-boggling maze. And now one of my first tests was to straighten it out.

I got to know Chuck, one of Pennsylvania's more prominent attorneys very well. He taught me more about labor law than I could have ever imagined. He also helped me to think like a lawyer (God forbid!). Slowly and painfully, we battled onward toward the creation of legal order in what the school district was doing and how it was doing it in the personnel arena. I hated every boring minute of it except for the martini sessions that Chuck and I often used to stimulate our brain cells when necessary. Finally, after about a year or so of revisions, reductions, refinements, and corrections, uniform and greatly condensed standards for personnel administration were brought into existence. These were hardly perfect, but they were drastically better than what had gone before.

CHAPTER 7

Unfortunately, my academic reverie as a law clerk was interrupted in the early 1980s by a contractual struggle with the secretaries' union. Traditionally, over many years, Upper Darby School Boards had treated this group of employees very poorly. Nobody took them too seriously. The school board's unfortunate mindset was that this was a union comprised primarily of women, just a bunch of glorified housewives. Negotiations were not going well. In fact there was no chance of a settlement. The school board's view was that the new teachers' contract had taken all the money. Here, take these crumbs; it's all we have to offer!

As the expiration of the old contract grew near, the secretaries' union decided to stop being doormats forever. About seventy of them showed up en masse at a public school board meeting. One of their leaders, an attractive, young African American woman identified herself as a union spokesperson. When she rose to speak in the public forum portion of the meeting, someone switched off the lights in the meeting room. Suddenly, seventy women were standing holding lit candles. Their leader tearfully spoke of dignity and fairness and equitable compensation in the workplace. It reminded me of a famous Papal Encyclical. It was awesome. The press wrote feverishly. It was an annihilation of school system management.

In the days that followed, news media articles and editorials chastised the school board for not negotiating fairly with the school system's secretaries and teacher assistants. Additionally, a series of very polite but on-point letters to the editor from union members appeared in the local press. The school district was embarrassed big time. A new contract was settled a few days later. Things quieted down quickly after that debacle. I always believed when it's over, it's over! What a silly notion!

Several months later, I was involved in a search for a new librarian at one of our middle schools. Superintendent Mike had told me to involve a committee at the school and get the best person. After a few weeks of interviews, I had the successful candidate sitting in my office at lunch time. She was previously a library assistant who had earned her degree as a school librarian. Quite a success story! The interview committee at the school loved her and recommended her for the job. I was in the process of having her sign the required papers when Superintendent Mike walked by the open door of my office, glared at my visitor for an instant, and then proceeded to his own quarters.

PERSONNEL ADVENTURES

One minute later, my meeting with the new librarian was interrupted by one of our secretaries. I was summoned to the superintendent's office. Now! I excused myself and went over to see Mike. He was sitting behind his desk, which he never did unless something really serious was afoot. Mike angrily inquired as to what in the hell "that woman" was doing sitting in my office. I went through the whole spiel regarding the successful search for a new librarian.

And then the roof caved in on my head. No, not the real roof, but the wrath of the boss! Now, I've told you lots of wonderful things about Mike as a leader. But he also had his negative sides. A nasty temper. An obsession with loyalty. And an inability to let bygones be bygones.

Mike issued an executive order with lots of vernacular trimming. Get "that woman" out of your office! Tell her she's not getting the librarian job because this superintendent will not recommend her for the required school board approval (public vote). Apparently, "that woman" had written one of those letters to the editor as a member of the secretaries' union during those ugly contract negotiations of the recent past. Mike had not forgotten, and he was well within his authority. "That woman" in his superintendent's opinion was disloyal and untrustworthy. This was not open to question by a subordinate.

Stupid me! I pleaded for executive mercy. I explained that I had just offered "that woman" the position. How could I go back on what I had just given. I bravely argued that writing a letter to the editor is a constitutional right. Bad mistake! Mike ranted and raved and tossed me out of his office with threats about consequences to me for my insubordination. This was serious business. For me, there was no way out.

I crawled back into my office like the lowly scum I was. I told "that woman" that she was not going to get the job she dreamed about. I groveled. She began crying. I began crying. I sent her on her way, destroyed and very unhappy. I'm just following orders from an imperial superintendent, like a loyal subject. A low point in my life. I prayed that I might get some chance to redeem myself with "that woman" in the future, but for the present, there were no other options. Sometimes you punt the football and hope for the best.

It took about a month for Mike and me to return to some kind of normalcy. He was really angry with me for quite some time. Thank heaven he

39

CHAPTER 7

began focusing on a new initiative. Mike had begun to utilize the services of a prominent education professor from the Philadelphia area to offer advice and counsel as a consultant to school district administrators.

The next few days would be personnel's turn with the professor. This prof was a bright elderly gentleman who had authored a number of books on educational administration. I looked forward to working with him and learning from him. The prof informed me that we would be traveling together to visit the personnel offices of a large corporation in downtown Philadelphia. Together, we would see what we could glean from the private sector to add to the school district's operations regarding personnel. We made arrangements to rendezvous the next day at a local hotel and drive together to the corporate building just a few minutes away on Market Street in Philly.

On the following morning, I picked up the professor and we drove into town. I parked right next to our target building, but the two of us could not seem to find a main entrance.

That's because there was none. We circled the building on foot several times and finally noticed a solid steel ground floor door where it appeared that employees were using plastic cards to gain admittance.

The prof suggested that we just follow any employee into the building when he or she had opened the door. Who was I to argue with someone from the halls of higher education? A young woman showed up with her plastic card in hand and opened the door. She apprehensively held the door open as the professor and I followed her in. The first floor entry area had no receptionist and was basically empty. Most curious, indeed, my dear Watson! The prof and I, just a pair of lost souls, followed the female employee onto the nearby elevator.

Just as soon as the elevator closed to take us up to places unknown, a siren began wailing. I thought it might be a fire alarm. But then a programmed voice kept repeating, "Red Alert, Intruders in the Building" over and over again. The prof hadn't quite figured it all out yet. But the woman employee and I got the picture. We both thought we were in trouble but for different reasons. Just as soon as the elevator door opened at its first stop, the young woman sprinted out screaming, "That's them! Get them!"

Armed company security guards with weapons drawn surrounded us. I prayed that they wouldn't shoot. The professor and I were roughly thrown against a wall and frisked. We weren't allowed to say a word. The Philly cops were on the way in force. Our female elevator companion was now crying hysterically, probably in shock. The old prof and I were prisoners, just a couple of hotshot corporate espionage agents. Some workers were hiding behind mainframe computers to avoid the shooting. It was all a wonderful visit to the funny farm.

Okay, so here's the bottom line: The professor had somehow mixed up the addresses of two very different buildings owned by the corporation. If you haven't guessed by now, we were in the wrong one. This was the company's high-security computer and records center—not open to outsiders. It took us about three hours of explaining and pleading with a host of Philadelphia detectives and corporation police to be set free.

When we finally were escorted into the fresh air, the prof was undeterred. He suggested that we visit the correct building the next day. Talk about an ivory tower approach! I respectfully declined. I had enough of Philly cops and corporate security to last me the rest of my life: "Yo! Doc! Did you happen to notice that we just missed being arrested or shot this morning!" I begged off. Smart administrators know when to punt. I headed back to the school district. When I returned, Mike asked me if I had learned a lot. More than you could ever imagine, I told him—an experience I'll always remember!

8

A STROKE OF FATE

During the early 1980s, under Mike's leadership, the Upper Darby School District gradually moved away from crisis management. The institutional rudder stabilized and education got back on course. The community grew more supportive, and the school system was enjoying labor-management peace. Administratively, we were actually focusing on instructional and curricular improvements for kids, and I was doing my best to tell the public all about it.

I thought that I had reached my pinnacle. I actually enjoyed my job. I knew that I was doing meaningful work in fostering communication and understanding between a large school system and its many publics. I had played a major role in cleaning up and streamlining the personnel area in the school system. I had even become much more enlightened academically after plodding through all the required academic courses for my doctorate at the University of Pennsylvania. I had come a long way from the streets of Philadelphia. I just wanted to be the best assistant superintendent that ever lived.

And then fate intervened. In the spring of 1984, Mike had some serious health problems. In fact, he had a mild stroke. And even though Mike bounced back from this adversity without any major paralysis or speech impediments, it was enough of a warning signal for him to realize that it would be best to vacate the superintendency. On October 1, 1984, Mike was granted a leave of absence until June 30, 1985, at which time he would retire. The school district suddenly had no superintendent.

The conventional wisdom is that a superintendent of schools should never be involved in picking his or her successor. But Mike never read that

CHAPTER 8

book. He didn't like things around him being left undone. Before he departed for the good life in sunny Palm Beach, he had thoroughly greased the skids with school board members and political powers. The new superintendent was locked in!

On February 12, 1985, the holy one who had been anointed with sacred oils was elected as only the sixth superintendent in the history of the Upper Darby School District. At forty-one years of age, I became the youngest superintendent to ever assume the reigns of power in the school system. I was unanimously appointed to a position that I had never sought. I was succeeding a superintendent who had had a stroke and who had obtained that position after his predecessor superintendent had had a heart attack. Doesn't do much for your confidence. I was numb. Being at the top involved challenges beyond my imagination. I was filled with self-doubt. It was the American Dream fulfilled. It was also the Nightmare of all Nightmares.

Before Mike left for Florida, he and I met together allegedly to reminisce about our many adventures together. However, Mike had a different agenda all planned out as usual. He smoothly shifted the conversation away from the nostalgic. An then his eyes filled up with tears.

"The truth of the matter is that you got this job because the powers that be believe that the devil you know is always better than the devil you don't know," Mike philosophized. "You're bright, and you'll be a great leader because you've already earned respect inside and outside this school system. But the most important asset for a school superintendent is a caring heart. That's why a diverse school system like this one needs you more than anyone else. You're the son that I never had and I've tried to be a good father, a good teacher. You've seen all of me, the strong and the weak sides. Use the best of me, whatever way you like. But be your own person and, damn it, believe in yourself and believe in this school community because they're believing in you."

No further words were uttered by either of us. That's because we were both all choked up with emotion and hugging one another. Mike bid adieu and departed forever. It was time to use the wealth of what Mike had taught me. It was time to start believing.

But to start off, I had something that had to be put right. It was the number one priority of my guilty conscience. The very first thing that I did as a new superintendent was to hire "that woman" whom Mike had blacklisted. "That woman" became a fine school librarian.

9

PHILOSOPHY DRIVES LEADERSHIP

One of the first telephone calls that I received after becoming superintendent of schools was from Guido, the neighborhood bookie when I was a kid. I hadn't heard from him or anyone else in my shady past for several years. I didn't return his repeated calls. And then I made the mistake of telling my wife Joan that Guido had called. She insisted that I talk to him. Honorable people don't forget their roots, she reasoned. I was being dishonorable, she chastised. Maybe so. But I was also afraid that Guido might want to set up gambling operations or some other illegal endeavor with my 1000 employees or even the students. Long-term wives, however, are supreme commanders in situations like this. I telephoned Guido the next day.

"Joey, can't you get out of this?" Guido inquired. "Sal and Rocco and me wuz thinkin' that it's always best to follow a son of a bitch into a job. Then whatever you do will be better than what went before. That guy Mike was too popular. The timing is bad. Just bag the whole thing!" Too late I told him. For better or worse, I was the new super.

"Well I guess we knew you were gonna do this thing no matter what we say so we all wish you the very best," Guido continued. His deep voice softened. "Sal and Rocco send their congratulations. We want to help. If there's anything you need, just holler. We want you to do well. We always knew you belonged at the top. You got the brains and the guts. Don't be ordinary, Joey. You only go around once in life, and it's a rarity that anyone who comes from

CHAPTER 9

where we come from ever gets this chance to do what you're gonna be doin'. We'll be rootin' for ya!"

When the conversation was over, I was overwhelmed with mixed feelings. What a schitzo I was. First, I won't talk to an old friend. And the next thing you know, I'm now fantasizing about being back with guys that common sense says I should avoid. Sal, Rocco, Guido, and Joey! The Musketeers reincarnated! Me as d'Artagnan! It would be us against the world! One for all and all for one! I longed for their companionship and support. I was alone at the top and I didn't like it.

I needed some working tools. Knives and guns were my first thought. Now, Joey, remember you're a distinguished educational leader. Use brain, not brawn. And so, in finest Socratic tradition, I put together my very own philosophy of educational administration to light my way in the darkness. It was developed from prolific academic reading while studying at Penn's Graduate School of Education, firsthand observation of a master superintendent (Mike), and some practical lessons from growing up in Philly. There was certainly nothing prescriptive about this menu. It was certainly not a how-to list. But it was a very firm set of beliefs and principles to guide my thinking and decision making regarding the million or so challenges I would face. That working philosophy went something like this:

- The most important task for a school superintendent is to consistently define and redefine his or her school system—what it believes, what it is trying to do, and why it deserves public support.
- Prioritize students in all planning and decision making. The best possible education for every kid is the target. Let nothing derail this objective.
- Recognize your feet of clay. Getting to be a superintendent does not bestow either omniscience or infallibility. Read prolifically. Be humble. Be flexible.
- Laugh at yourself. And never be afraid to admit a mistake.
- Timely and honest communication with all of your constituencies (especially the school board) is a key to effective leadership. It is also critical to survival in the superintendency.
- Do not try to solve problems alone. Co-opt key players into dilemmas to make solutions ours, not yours. Delegate. Complex problems should be layered to uncomplicate them.

- Give your administrative staff and especially school principals plenty of rope. Encourage them to take risks and try new things. Always take time to listen to people and their ideas. Support! Encourage! Praise!
- Give credit where credit is due. Sharing the spotlight is the mark of a great leader.
- Credibility cannot be built in time of crisis. You establish your integrity and principle on a daily basis through a thousand different interactions.
- Fighting teacher unions is a formula that nets disaster. Find common ground, compromise, and work together.
- You will never win fights with people who buy ink by the barrel (the news media), so don't try. Newspapers and television stations are in the business of making money. You don't have to like what they do. You do have to find a way to live with it.
- It is true that money cannot solve problems by itself, but it is also true that money almost always makes the difference! Money matters in education. Fight to get it for your students and your schools.

An effective superintendent of schools is first and foremost a philosopher. Through the myriad of decisions and problems and trials and tribulations that I had to face during fourteen years as a superintendent, my best weapon was a strongly held philosophy. School leaders need their own set of firm beliefs about public school administration that can be applied to the complicated day-to-day dilemmas as well as the maze of unforeseen situations that grow out of running a people business.

10

THE VISIBILITY FACTOR

The hard reality is that a superintendent of schools functions under a public microscope. Educational leaders should dance under the magnifying glass rather than trying to shun it. If you've got high visibility by the nature of your job, then why not use it?

The most obvious bully pulpit for a superintendent of schools is the monthly public school board meeting. From 1985 through 1999, I was present at 400 consecutive sessions of our school directors. Getting sick or being under the weather was something I did not permit myself.

At each and every one of those school board meetings, I began offering some public commentary that helped to accent and define whatever was happening in the school system. I shared the floor with central administrators and school principals and teachers in presentations on curriculum and instruction initiatives, staff development programs, pupil services interventions, and special education matters.

None of this was well received at first. Some school board members were anxious to get on with their traditional bantering about budgets, buses, and buildings. Citizens who came to the meeting with specific agendas to complain about were impatient. News reporters were bored: why were we talking about education at a school board meeting?

But I was a junkyard dog. I wouldn't let go. And eventually the public meeting culture changed for the better. School board members began listening to the educational presentations and asking questions. Reporters began

CHAPTER 10

writing. Administrators and teachers gained credibility and praise for what they were doing. As for the citizen grinches and disgruntled taxpayers, they always despised these programs about education at school board meetings. They were enemies. I could have cared less about what they wanted!

During the era of public education bashing which spanned most of my career as a superintendent, I also utilized the school board meeting as my forum to fight back against corporate and political misinformation campaigns nationally. This was an unheard-of practice for a local school superintendent to go on record at public school board meetings against powerful figures and forces attacking public education. Some of my staff and many superintendent colleagues forecast my demise because of this outspokenness, which was now getting play in the local press. But I was undaunted. Leadership is about standing up for what is right regardless of the consequences.

One unexpected outcome of my public posturing is that my relationship with the working press was dramatically enhanced. Perhaps the news group on the Upper Darby beat just admired a theoretically suicidal superintendent intent on ending his career. But I rather think that they found a stand-up leader in education to be refreshing. This is not to say that I had some wonderful relationship with the news media. But the more I talked with reporters, the more rapport I built and that proved to be quite useful in times of crisis when candor and mutual understanding were required.

I estimate that I attended more than 1,400 school district events during my 14 years as a superintendent, never wasting an opportunity to chat with parents and community residents on each of those occasions. I also delivered about 600 formal speeches on educational issues inside and outside the community to friend and foe alike. And I authored many commentary pieces in area newspapers to establish the school system's programs, positions, and initiatives. Whether this practice gained respect or made enemies for me is not what's important here. What I was doing was all about issues, not about me. Leaders speak out on matters that matter! And shrinking-violet closet dwellers do not belong in the superintendent's chair.

My wife Joan and I chose to reside in the Upper Darby School District during all the years of my superintendency. This is a controversial topic with many school superintendents. For me, it was a no-brainer. As the educational leader of the Upper Darby School District community, I was going to be a part of that community. In walking the neighborhood with Joan, shopping locally, wolfing down hundreds of pancakes at civic fund-raising breakfasts, attending a variety of local cocktail parties, and sometimes (though not often) hosting unexpected parent/student/community visitors, I clarified more issues, put out more fires, built more understanding, and solved more real-world problems than could have ever occurred in the formal setting of the administration building. In the superintendency, nothing beats personal contact. For me, living in the middle of my school community was a respect builder.

Inside the district's twelve schools, I was a periodic visitor, popping into classrooms to chat with teachers and pupils and get the feel of a hundred different learning environments. More important, I was a superintendent who regularly guest taught classes. My poetry classes at the elementary level were my specialty, but I did my teaching thing at all levels. There is no better way to observe students firsthand and best understand what teachers do every day.

With school principals, I never wanted to be viewed as a threatening overseer. Whenever I visited a school I listened and supported and encouraged and praised. The principals and teachers responded by doing marvelous things. Today, there is tremendous, well-deserved community pride for the public schools in Upper Darby.

I was always very quick to publicly honor significant accomplishments of students and staff at public meetings of the school board. But beyond that, I sent literally thousands of personal congratulatory notes to pupils and faculty when some educational success event took place. I brought high-achieving and award-winning students to the administration building for breakfasts and luncheons. I hosted a hundred receptions for teachers in my office.

I spent thousands of dollars of my own money, taking students on unique field trips (e.g., treating outstanding music achievers to a night of opera at an Italian restaurant in South Philadelphia), and buying twenty bottles of champagne for my maintenance workers laboring heroically to get a school open after a fire. I also set up my own personally funded scholarship, which has been awarded to a deserving Upper Darby High School graduate for the past seventeen years.

Finally, way back in 1985, I was looking for some way to better communicate to our many publics that we were an achieving school system. That's because the comparative standardized test score results issued by the state

CHAPTER 10

each year were lousy barometers of educational quality. The Upper Darby School District was doing an outstanding job in educating one of the most diverse populations of students in the Greater Philadelphia area, but standardized test results would never show our hundreds of success stories with kids that went way beyond successfully filling in bubble sheets.

We needed to get past test scores to different kinds of external validations of the richness of our educational quality. And so I dictated (something I rarely did) that the Upper Darby School District would become much more open to qualitative evaluations from the outside than ever before. We would build and learn from professional visitations to our schools. Additionally, I mandated our schools to enter available academic competitions to a greater extent than ever before.

Not everyone embraced this strategy. Some administrators and teachers naively thought it wasn't necessary. This new openness of schools to external scrutiny was threatening to the comfortable status quo. Others were simply afraid to fail.

I remember the high school science department teacher leaders telling me that the Delaware County Science Fair competition was "beneath their dignity." I blew a fuse. Upper Darby High's science department was asleep at the wheel. Meanwhile, a neighboring parochial high school was sweeping up all of the annual science awards at this event and attaining widespread publicity for its superb teaching of science. I'm not sure whether this was just a lack of initiative or apprehension over how well Upper Darby's science students might do at this fair. However, I was not offering options here. We would compete like never before.

The following year, Upper Darby High School students dominated the science fair competition with numerous winning entries. This was the beginning of a flood of solid showings over many years by our kids in competitions in music, the arts, business, vocational, engineering, history, mathematics, and many other areas. It wasn't that we always won, but rather that we proved to our students and our community that we would and could be competitive with all other schools in things academic and beyond.

Oh, and one final note. I also traveled through the schools stressing the need for more intensive research by our own people about what works in public schools. And I began actively seeking out and empowering risk takers to innovate and implement new programs. It was all about stirring up change and improvement and many staff people began buying in. I handed out footballs to lots of folks and told them to run for the goal line. We scored many touchdowns!

Today, the Upper Darby School District derives great self-esteem and pride from the numerous national, state, and private sector honors and awards it has garnered in open competition: Six National Blue Ribbon Schools of Excellence (among twelve schools) and citations from the Commonwealth of Pennsylvania for exemplary programs in staff development, drug prevention, the arts, and school business partnerships. Indeed, visitors have come from all over the world to view Upper Darby's unique educational climate in a school district with a comprehensive curriculum that extends to all pupils.

Among Upper Darby's most progressive innovations are an outstanding teacher center that has retrained and enhanced the expertise of hundreds of its own staff as well as professionals from many other public and parochial schools; a model centralized early childhood kindergarten center; a spectacular performing arts center, a joint project between Upper Darby Township and the school system, that has exponentially expanded cultural and theatrical opportunities for students and community; and one of Greater Philadelphia's largest Sponsor a Scholar Programs, an initiative that pairs up Upper Darby High School financially needy seniors with adult mentors and eventual scholarship assistance from corporate sponsors.

Paul Houston, the Executive Director of the American Association of School Administrators, has referred to the superintendency as a vocational calling, much more than just a CEO job. He is absolutely correct. Being a superintendent of schools involves highly visible missionary work, spiritual conviction, spreading a gospel, and converting others in the most visible of environments.

11

ABOUT SCHOOL BOARDS AND FOOD

Whenever I attended national conventions of school superintendents, I was always fascinated by the obsessive cocktail party talk about perpetual clashes of superintendents with their school boards. I really must have missed the boat on this one. I had nothing to add to these conversations of bad-mouthing school board members.

Talk about being out of the mainstream. There I was with forty-nine different elected school directors over my fourteen years as a superintendent. They came with forty-nine unique personalities and sometimes with their own eccentricities. Worse yet, the Upper Darby School Board by its own design rotated its presidency and vice presidency leadership positions every two years. According to the conventional wisdom of school superintendents, this should have been a disaster for me. But it wasn't.

My school boards stood shoulder to shoulder with me in a hundred difficult public situations. They always listened respectfully to me as well as the other administrators and teachers that I brought before them. Of course, they didn't always agree with everything the administration presented, but why should any superintendent of schools expect rubber stamping from thinking people?

At times, I argued passionately and lost. Get over it! The working relationship was the thing. Superintendents are supposed to recommend initiatives and improvements. However, chief executive officers are not divinely anointed. And very few school system matters are of a life-or-death caliber.

CHAPTER 11

You don't have to like every person with whom you work. But superintendents do need to establish some common ground with each and every one of them. That requires flexibility, a relentless positive attitude, patience, and time.

My school boards and I hardly agreed on everything! Many times, I humbly buried my ego. I tried to respect each individual no matter whether or not we differed on some issue. And most important, I honored the board's collective wisdom, its myriad of viewpoints that eventually ended up in a consensus.

Years later, in lecturing to graduate students about the internal politics of school systems, there were always abundant questions about my remarkable success with my school boards. My school district was a dynamic leader in innovative educational programs because the school board had handed out so many green lights in supporting numerous changes and innovations in curriculum and instruction. During my years as superintendent, we were perpetually involved in bond issues for expansion construction at our schools to house our growing student population. In a fiscal climate of tight money, my school boards never blinked on approving the borrowing for these projects. And because of the state's abdication of its responsibility to pay its fair share of the costs of basic instruction during the 1990s, my school boards were annually increasing real estate taxes. How had I ever survived? In the graduate schools, I always tell these aspiring administrators that it was all in the food.

Actually, the action was really in the rapport and mutual respect being incrementally built and then fostered between the school board and its administration with the superintendent as key player. But such long-standing relationships of trust are not easy to establish in sterile board rooms or over telephones. In leadership dynamics, dinners and luncheons and breakfasts are catalytic converters that translate formality, reserve, and anal-retentive stuffiness into honest exchanges of views and concerns.

Whenever individual board members would call me with something about which they were upset, I tried to steer them into a luncheon or breakfast at my treat. At the very least, I would get them into my office to discuss their issues over coffee and pastry. And sometimes the kitchen inside my home became the meeting place. Meaningful communication needs eye contact and facial expressions and body language. And food tends to soften many a situation. If something's that important to someone, a one-dimensional telephone is not a great working tool.

Prior to each monthly Upper Darby School District board meeting, the president and vice president would meet with me to formulate an agenda. I always made sure this was done over food. Breakfast or lunch in a local diner. Or deli sandwiches in an administration building conference room. The point being that serious planning and interacting are best done face-to-face.

Annually, the board and its administration would always go away together on one weekend for an in-depth planning retreat. Lots of heavy stuff went down at these sessions. Hard looks by all of us at our school system, what we were accomplishing, what we needed to change, and where we needed to be going. Food was central to all of this. Great buffet breakfasts and luncheons between meetings at which board members and administrators got to know each other as human beings. And gala evening dinners, at which we hosted prominent experts who came with ideas for a give-and-take about improving public education.

School board–administration relationships are often what the superintendent makes them. Honesty, straightforward communication, and recognition of the authority of an elected school board are underlying premises for a superintendent to build camaraderie and unity of purpose among a school system's leadership family.

Finally, I would be remiss if I did not tell you about the spectacular annual dinners that my wife Joan orchestrated for the school board and the administration and all of their spouses during the Christmas holidays each year. Each year Joan would get more and more crazy about the food. Four or five gourmet entrees for fifty people to go with six or seven different appetizers and four to five separate desserts. And heaven forbid we should use caterers or buy prepared food. We cooked together like lunatic chefs for days in advance of each year's party. A married couple on a survival mission. Everything made from scratch. No shortcuts for Joan. Tons of food. Astounding feasts. A necessary commitment for our school community.

Every year I would tell the visitors to our home that "a guest in our house is God in our house." The food was truly from heaven. But much more important, the personal contact and human understanding between school

CHAPTER 11

board members and administrators that grew from these six- to seven-hour extravaganzas were invaluable. It unified us as a family with a central purpose: the best education for Upper Darby's kids!

School boards are all about respect, for each other and for their administration, teachers, support staff, students, parents, and community at large. But they also deserve respect. School boards exemplify the purest form of public service. It has been my privilege to know some of the most incredible giving people as Upper Darby school directors, and today I still number many of them among my good friends.

12

THE ARRANGED MARRIAGE

Truth be told, my wife Joan and I had an arranged marriage. Back in 1961, Joan's grandmother and my mother plotted the whole thing out. They were close friends and had decided that Joan and I would make a perfect married couple.

When my mother told me I should meet this very pretty and intelligent girl who was the granddaughter of a friend of hers, I immediately turned off the channel. I could only imagine what sort of disaster case this handpicked young woman would be. No way I was getting involved with some female chosen for me by my mother.

For about six months, my mother nagged me incessantly about the opportunity I was missing. I still wasn't buying. So Joan's grandmother and my mother orchestrated an accidental meeting between Joan and me at my home. It all worked like a charm. Joan was invited to accompany my mother to some cultural event. The timing was carefully synchronized to make sure that I would be at home. Joan showed up at our house to pick up my mother. When I answered the door, I immediately fell in love with the most beautiful girl I had ever seen. It was an on-the-spot knockout. I was badly smitten. It was a perfectly executed plan!

You should first of all know that Joan is extremely bright. When I was courting her, we often met at the University of Pennsylvania library. I just wanted to look at her and be with her. I always pretended to be studying from various books in front of me, but my heart was fluttering and my brain was

CHAPTER 12

slush. Joan, however, was always a serious student. I remember her reading books written in French in order to obtain prime source information about Slavic history, in which she had great interest. It was awesome. I despaired at the time. How would a guy like me ever get to first base with someone this intelligent? Well, miracles do happen. Especially because this magnetism turned out to be a mutual thing. We were truly made for one another.

Now, some forty years later, Joan and I are still very married and still very much in love. We have had wonderful joys and experiences in our life together. And Joan has been my strength through a thousand different school system crises.

I could never stand being away from Joan. Early in our marriage, I was in New Orleans without her while working for La Salle College. Our basketball team played its game on a Saturday night and I filed the required news coverage with the Philly papers. Ordinarily, the La Salle group would have headed home in the morning. But the next day was Super Bowl Sunday and the game was going to be played right there in New Orleans. The La Salle entourage had obtained game tickets for each member of our traveling party. Everyone was very excited. All except me! I was in love. I gave away my precious Super Bowl ticket and grabbed a 7:00 A.M. flight out of New Orleans at Sunday's sunrise. Later that afternoon, I watched the Super Bowl on television snuggled up to my beloved Joan back in Philly. That's the way our marriage was and still is!

Joan is the purest, kindest, and most decent person I have ever met. She's had a very successful career mostly working for environmental protection causes, but I've always been her number one project. Whether I needed loving, nurturing, counseling, understanding, massaging, or just a good straightening out, she has always been there for me. My Joan, the love of my life!

By the nature of the job, a superintendent of schools needs a special someone. It's far too solitary at the top no matter how many superficial acquaintances surround you in the workplace. That special someone might be one very close friend or a lover or a spouse. Whatever the case, a special someone by your side is an invaluable asset. The superintendency is not something you want to face alone!

A VISIT FROM THE FBI

Sometime in November of 1994, I received a telephone call from an FBI agent. I thought it was some sort of practical joke. It wasn't. An appointment was made for two FBI agents to come to my office to discuss a very serious matter the next morning. That's all that I was told.

In true paranoiac fashion, I immediately thought about fleeing the country. Undoubtedly, my past had caught up with me. I would be arrested for knowing Sal and Guido and Rocco. My career as a school superintendent would end in disgrace.

One of my assistant superintendents at the time was Jim. He was in charge of the curriculum and instruction areas of our administration. Jim was a marvelous school administrator, a former elementary principal truly at his best with little kids, an innovative risk taker, and most important a diplomat. Whenever a situation at a school grew beyond the capability of the school principal to handle, Jim put out the fires. He was a master at handling complex problems that involved teachers, students, and parents.

Jim was also my confidant. I told him about the pending FBI visit and the usually unflappable Jim turned pale as a ghost. I told him not to worry about me. His reply was most surprising. Jim said that it wasn't me that he was worried about! That's because Jim was certain that the FBI was after Gil and him!

Gil was Jim's best friend. Gil was also the outstanding principal at Upper Darby High School for most of the years of my superintendency. Gil ran one

CHAPTER 13

of Pennsylvania's largest and most diverse high schools with an iron fist but a gentle heart. The school accomplished wondrous things under his leadership.

Back in the previous summer, Jim and Gil had asked me if they could go hunting for elk in Montana for a few days in October when school was in session. Since all the school administrators were on twelve-month work years, vacations could theoretically be taken at any time, although out of practicality most administrators used up their vacation days in the summers.

However, this was a one-time opportunity for Jim and Gil. They had actually won the right to hunt through a Montana lottery conducted by the state's fish and game bureau. I okayed their vacation requests. And for a few days in October they were gone. That's all I knew.

Now in my office, Jim explained what he was so upset about. He and Gil had lived on a ranch for three days out in Montana eating mooseburgers and venison stew and bear steaks cooked by the rancher's wife. They hunted each day, came up empty-handed except for one white-tailed deer, but were having the time of their lives. Then, on the final night, before their departure, Gil and Jim were invited by their host to attend a real town meeting. They readily agreed. This would be fun. A cultural experience.

My two school administrators rode with the rancher in his pickup truck into the tiny wilderness town. When they arrived at the high school, fifty more small trucks were parked outside with rifles in gun racks in full view behind the front seat of each vehicle. Lots of cowboy types were strolling into the high school auditorium for the meeting. Gil and Jim and the rancher followed them in.

The first speaker offered his advice on the stockpiling of food and choosing assorted weapons and ammunition. The second expert focused on the best places to shoot a human enemy in order to put them out of commission in a hurry. And the feature presenter of the evening spoke at length about being watchful for the black helicopters that would signal the government takeover in the near future. There was also some explanation about the most effective use of walkie talkies in battle and the utilization of reflective blankets to hide persons and materials from enemy planes flying overhead.

By now you've probably figured it out. Gil and Jim were involuntary attendees at one of those infamous militia meetings held in the far west. An evening in a cuckoo nest with many deranged birds. Jim was convinced that

A VISIT FROM THE FBI

the FBI had caught Gil and him on film and wanted to question them as radical militants. Jim said that he'd be happy to never see Montana again.

And so on a memorable November night in 1994, neither Gil nor Jim nor I got any sleep. For different reasons, we each expected to soon be captives of the FBI.

When the agents arrived at the administration building in the morning, they created quite a stir. The two trench coated individuals presented their FBI credentials at the receptionist's desk with flourish. Word circulated fast. FBI agents in the school district. It was better than a good action movie.

Well, things are never as bad as they seem to be. It turned out that the two agents were not after Gil or Jim or me. They were routinely investigating a charge of alleged child molestation. And best of all, it had nothing to do with anything going on inside the school system. The feebies were following up on a divorce situation of one of my male teachers whose wife had accused him of all sorts of nasty stuff with his own children. Talk about ugly domestic separations. Ordinarily I would have been horrified. But today all I could feel was relief! I was giddy!

The agents wanted access to the personnel records of the teacher under investigation. I telephoned our labor attorney on the spot, and he advised that we comply with the FBI request. I turned over the files. Not surprisingly, there was nothing of any value to the criminal investigation. But the FBI agents were most appreciative of the school system's cooperation. They left satisfied. I collapsed on my office coach and took time to smell the flowers.

Nothing much more happened after that. But rumors flew for months. That afternoon, Jim and Gil and I went out for drinks. We all needed to calm down. In school administration, you're only as good as your next crisis. Tomorrow always brings new challenges and problems to overcome. The three of us joked a lot about Montana. But we avoided discussing the FBI. Their visit had been enough for a lifetime!

14

MY STUDENTS

The egalitarian nature of America's public schools is not clearly understood in America's circles of power. But then whoever said that government bureaucrats and politicians and corporate leaders were very bright? Too many of these pontificating sophomores are clueless indeed.

In the view of so many of these self-appointed, alleged national experts on education, students in public schools are widgets rolling down an assembly line. Just pour learning potion into their empty heads and each should come out perfectly. What widgets? The reality is that there was no assembly line in my Upper Darby School District, only heterogeneity—certainly not homogenized white bread.

Sure, I had plenty of highly motivated students who had strong backing from the home and were academically strong. But I also had substantial numbers of community children who came from dysfunctional homes. They brought lots of baggage and problems to the classroom. The diverse Upper Darby School District community was also characterized by significant annual populations of newcomer pupils who brought with them a host of educational needs. It was all about families looking for the promised land in Upper Darby's affordable housing and good schools. Hundreds of students transferred into the system from nearby Philadelphia each year. So too did many more pupils from all around the United States and in fact the world. One of my schools featured more than forty different first-generation nationalities being absorbed into America.

CHAPTER 14

My school system also enrolled one of the larger populations of special education students in Pennsylvania. These pupils had a wide variety of social, emotional, physical, and learning needs. And, finally, my schools also had numbers of students who were thrown out of or asked to leave parochial or private schools. All of this challenged my teaching staff to the outer limits.

One size fits all? Really? In curriculum and instruction? Or with standardized tests that adequately evaluate individual differences? You must be kidding. My students were literally all over the place. Someone must have mixed up the order for perfect raw materials to make our perfect widgets.

Instead, I had thousands of uniquely individual students with thousands of different needs. It's the beauty of egalitarianism. Teaching all kinds of kids with all kinds of educational challenges. It's the most underrated thing about public education. And it's what's most ignored and least understood by public school bashers all across our nation.

Early on in my superintendency, the Pennsylvania Department of Education initiated a series of standardized tests to boldly tell the Commonwealth's citizens which schools were getting the job done and which ones weren't. Test results were issued for every school and school district in the state. Political accountability for schools? More like a trainload of highly publicized nonsense.

Surprise, surprise! Schools that served advantaged, upper-class, primarily white communities looked really good on these tests. Most urban schools handling the most disadvantaged kids in the Commonwealth looked bad. And schools like mine with a conglomeration of diversity came out mediocre; we had student test results scattered all over the universe.

This state program was a despicable misuse of testing and a forerunner of the epidemic of many similar brainless efforts that still dominate the public education scene in America today. The news media made it all even worse by giving it credence. I sent a letter to the state's bureaucrats. I tried to be academic. Here's just a part of what I wrote:

> The true extent of what any school does to teach and meet the needs of its students and families can hardly be evaluated from your school by school comparison test results. In presenting this picture to the public, you have ignored many significantly different characteristics among individual schools and communities. Many factors can influence the differences among schools in

standardized test results, including community density, size of schools, the extent of socioeconomic diversity in the school's community, the mobility of the pupil population (annual transfers into and out of the schools every year); curriculum articulation and resources, numbers of marginal English language proficiency pupils, and the degree of financial support for the schools.

Such variables can cause the statistical portraits of two schools or two school systems to be dramatically different. To attribute the ensuing test score contrasts of one school versus another unilaterally to the quality of education being offered is a highly questionable conclusion.

School districts that serve diverse communities of students with very mixed needs, abilities, and aspirations are done a great disservice when their standardized test scores are used by the state to paint their educational efforts as inferior. You have essentially classified and arranged Pennsylvania's schools into caste system judgments via test scores. You should know better than to do this!

I waited several weeks for anyone in Harrisburg to respond. When no one did, I went public, rewriting my letter into a guest editorial that was published in the *Philadelphia Inquirer*. That attracted the Pennsylvania Department of Education's attention at last.

Shortly thereafter, some self-important state bureaucrat telephoned to tell me that I didn't know what I was talking about. He alleged that I was just avoiding accountability. I asked him how he would know anything about accountability since like most Harrisburg bureaucrats, he was far removed from any personal contact with the general public. The conversation got nastier. I accented our discussion by asking him how long he had had his lobotomy. He responded by threatening to take my superintendent's commission away from me. I countered by promising to visit his office to settle our differences. That ended our dialogue. For the future, I decided to ignore the state bureaucracy as much as possible. No intelligent life on that planet.

Academic argumentation has never impressed me. I needed a new strategy. So to help my school community better understand this state debacle, I held a public meeting with an audience of teachers and parents. Together we brainstormed some portraits of the Upper Darby School District student body. I reasoned that if all of us could more clearly see our kids as individuals, it would be much easier to grasp the fact that they were human beings, not widgets, and that any composite test score portraits really didn't tell

CHAPTER 14

much at all except that these were young people with very different needs. The resultant egalitarian Upper Darby student body looked something like this:

- Emily Excellent: High-achieving college prep student with strong family backing; a shining star in and out of the classroom.
- Randy Rising Star: Comes from a difficult socioeconomic background. He is performing well academically and is involved in extracurricular activities.
- Self-fulfilling Prophecy Phil: Comes from a tough socioeconomic background. He is performing poorly, uninvolved in school activities and barely surviving academically.
- Freddie Fast Lane: Has the right stuff in terms of intelligence and family support but is obsessed with hard rock, video games, drugs, and the opposite sex. Average to poor academic success.
- Nelly Newcomer: Immigrant pupil or upwardly mobile transfer student. Determined to succeed through hard work. Struggles to achieve and does so. Good family support.
- Urban Sally: Recent transfer student into the Upper Darby School District from Philadelphia. A tenth-grader with a fifth-grade reading level. Trying her best, but running uphill.
- Tommy Transfer: Newcomer who has been expelled or pushed out of a private/parochial school. Brings a suitcase full of trouble to his new school.
- Teresa Transfer: Newcomer who with her parents' concurrence has transferred from a private/parochial school. Doing well academically and very involved in school activities.
- Albert Average: Non-college-prep, middle-of-the-road kid. Never gets much notice. Regularly attends school but avoids the spotlight. Uninvolved in school activities. Unsure of career goals.
- Allisa Average: Non-college-prep, middle-of-the-road kid. Has found her niche in vocational education. Doesn't test well, but regularly demonstrates a unique set of technical skills in school. Headed for community college and beyond.
- Debbie Difficulty: Discipline problem who's always in and out of trouble. Pleads innocence whenever caught. All of her trouble is

caused by the unfair school environment. No academic priorities for this young lady.
- Sammy Slow Learner: Below average IQ. Mainstreamed into the school population. Walks the academic tightrope.
- David Deprived: Youngster from a terrible home environment. Two strikes against him. Yet he's getting better than average grades in a tech prep engineering program.
- Jimmy Jekyll: Student who is emotionally disturbed. Has been in and out of mental hospital. Uses prescribed medication for control, but can explode at any time.

This sample list represents just some of the pupils who inhabited my school system. And this exercise could probably go on ad infinitum. Such a list would never be all inclusive. Nor would it be scientific. And categorizing kids was hardly the purpose of this activity. Nevertheless, generating a matrix like the one above was a very effective way to focus on the diversity of my school system's pupil population.

It was a wonderful teaching tool because it made people think. I can't tell you how many times I engaged parent groups, teachers, and community organizations in analytical discussions of children and instructional approaches in our schools. It was also an incredibly valuable primer for the school board, the nine elected officials overseeing the school system. It helped all of us to concentrate on the reality that our student body had a diverse set of needs and that no two schools or school districts are alike. We needed a myriad of teaching and learning strategies, not another testing program. And we had to love and care about students as unique individuals, not widgets.

Years ago, there was a television show about New York called *The Naked City*. Its opening line every week was that there were eight million stories in The Naked City. Well, in the Upper Darby School District when I was superintendent of schools, there were ten thousand stories in the Upper Darby school system city!

Ironically, in Upper Darby, like most school districts in Pennsylvania, school system standardized testing programs had been in place for many years to determine individual students strengths and weaknesses in basic subjects and to help classroom teachers better know their pupil needs.

CHAPTER 14

Parents were always apprised of the individual test results for their children each year.

So what could be a more senseless practice than testing kids into oblivion with yet another set of standardized tests? But that's just what the Pennsylvania bureaucracy did, subsequently leading the public to fallacious statewide comparisons of schools using test results of very different student populations as evaluations of alleged school quality. It was all a misguided state plan to "club the schools to greatness" with standardized tests held over the heads of students, teachers, and school administrators. Not exactly Pennsylvania's finest hour, but then state government in the Commonwealth has never had too many fine hours anyway.

The great American author Jonathan Kozol has summarized the points that I am trying to make far better than I could ever hope to do. He has written, "There is a pathological madness to the punitive motif that drives this strange obsession with repetitive empirical assessment" (*Education Week*, November 14, 2001)." High-stakes standardized-test bludgeoning has no place in American education. The billions of dollars spent each year on this farce throughout the United States could be much better utilized for smaller class sizes, universal preschool education, remedial and enrichment courses, teacher training, and a host of other worthwhile projects.

15

THE SLUSH FUND

Being a superintendent of schools at a public school board meeting is not usually much fun. That's because you often become the public's dartboard at a spirited town meeting. Our democratic republic in action can be a painful experience. On many of these occasions, you take some shots. And sometimes you get bulls-eye skewered.

I had only been a superintendent a few weeks when I got my first public beating. Nothing too serious, just a bunch of disgruntled citizens complaining about their school taxes and extending their wrath to the rest of the school universe. Now if you're not used to skewering it can be excruciatingly painful. Best to bite your tongue during public attacks. No sense making things worse. The public barrage soon ended. But then the local press immortalized the evening with a hyperbolized account completely blown out of all proportion to reality. Every superintendent should have an underground bunker for these occasions!

When the next school board meeting rolled around, I was very apprehensive. This dartboard stuff could get real tired in a hurry! My wounds from the previous month were still healing. And then suddenly a few minutes before the session was about to begin, I saw Rocco, of all people in the back of the boardroom. I bolted from my chair and sprinted to the rear of the room. I hugged the ponytailed, black-haired Rocco, someone I hadn't seen in many years, and quickly asked him what he was doing at an Upper Darby School Board meeting.

CHAPTER 15

Rocco's answer was chilling. The word was that Joey needed help. Essentially, Sal had ordered Rocco to straighten out any public attackers of me after the meeting. Sal and Rocco had obviously read about the last meeting when I was publicly blistered. Simple solution: Identify these bitchers and moaners and convince them to stay home and watch television on school board meeting nights! Rocco was ready to terrorize anyone "takin' off on Joey!" I nearly fainted on the spot. There was little time to dissuade Rocco from his mission. The meeting was about to start. I sprinted back to my seat at the board table. I was now sweating droplets of fear.

Well, one thing about school board meetings. They are never predictable. Contrary to last month's pandemonium, that evening's business was orderly and peaceful. No public attacks. No debate. The session over in twenty minutes. Rocco just glaring. No enemies to dispose of! I said goodbye to my old friend. He told me not to worry—he'd be back! I knew I had to do something, but what?

A few days later, I traveled back to the old neighborhood after work. Having an appointment with a gang leader in the back of a Catholic Church is something very few school superintendents have ever done. Lucky me! After we renewed acquaintances and reminisced a bit about the days of our impetuous youth, I begged Sal to back off, to let me sink or swim on my own as a superintendent of schools. Finally, Sal agreed to call off Rocco, but he was visibly disappointed. There must be something else he could do for an old buddy? He wanted to help. This was not something I should gloss over. Sal headed for the front of the church to light some votive candles. It gave me time to think. My mind raced. And then I remembered that my guidance counselors and social workers were constantly coming across families and students with severe financial needs.

There were heartbreaking stories of good kids who weren't able to participate in nominal-cost activities because of economic circumstances at home. We had young people who couldn't afford the cost of the SAT or opportunistic enrichment courses at area universities or educational field trips or a host of school activities like the senior prom. We also had students with health needs unattended because of being poor. We had pupils who sometimes needed shoes or coats or whatever. I laid all of this on Sal.

I told him that I had been toying with the idea of establishing a private fund to address as many of these needs as possible on an anonymous basis. This of course wasn't true, but the more I talked about it, the better it sounded. Talk about touching the lives of kids in need. Unfortunately, Sal didn't seem to be too interested.

Rocco was standing in the back of the church with Sal's bodyguards. Sal kissed me on both cheeks and exited the church with his entourage. At least I wouldn't have to worry about disgruntled citizens at Upper Darby School Board meetings having to be accountable to Rocco in the future.

Two days later, when I arrived at work in the administration building shortly after 7:00 A.M., I found a plain white envelope on my desktop. The typewritten lettering on the envelope said: "To: Joey's Fund For Needy Kids. From: An Anonymous Donor." Inside was one thousand dollars in ten dollar bills. No other message accompanied the money. I hesitated only for about a millisecond. Enough already! I wasn't about to worry about where the money came from or make a big thing about it. The Superintendent's Student Assistance Fund was born that morning.

Years ago, there was a television show called *The Millionaire*. Its weekly stories were all the same. Some good person was desperate for money. The Millionaire sent his representative to solve the dilemma and save the day. It was all done anonymously.

Essentially, I used the same model in doling out financial assistance to students with the most serious needs. Of course, I was handing out gifts much smaller than one million dollars. But in all my years as a school superintendent, nothing ever felt better. And boy did it ever warm my heart. Watchful administrators in my schools would call a student's money problem to my attention. And then I would make something possible that was impossible for some deserving young person.

As time went on, word quietly spread throughout the school system regarding the wonderful Superintendent's Student Assistance Fund. Fresh donations came in periodically from alumni, teachers, and administrators, school board members, small business owners, and a host of others. And I never had to deny a worthy request.

So there you have it. Mysterious seed money for the best of purposes inspires more of the same altruistic action by many others. Whatever works. Always believe in angels. Always have faith in the goodness of caring people.

16

THE SILENCE OF THE SHEPHERDS

It was 1988. I was a veteran school superintendent, having survived four years at the helm. I had taken the day off to attend a funeral. Sal's dad had died after a prolonged bout with lung cancer and was being buried later that morning. And so I sat with Sal and Rocco and Guido having breakfast in the legendary Melrose Diner in South Philly at 7:30 A.M. We were all eating spicy, hot Italian sausage and peppers with scrambled eggs smothered in tomato gravy. Not exactly your basic WASP morning cuisine.

I hadn't seen my old friends in almost two years. I wondered why we hadn't done this more often. Maybe I was becoming too respectable, afraid to be seen with these guys. Did it really take a funeral to help me remember that these were my people? The ones that I grew up with. The ones who were there when I needed help the most.

We were actually talking about the Upper Darby School District. I was telling Sal about a very bright Asian American thirteen-year-old student whom I had been able to send to a seminar on molecular biology at a university in Iowa thanks to the Student Assistance Fund that had been established by an anonymous donor. I expressed delight regarding the influx of so many immigrants from Southeast Asia into the school system. I stressed how much I admired the work ethic, academic priority, and family structure of those students.

Sal, Rocco, and Guido listened attentively as I noted that the school system pupil population was growing again. I had been able to gain school

CHAPTER 16

board approval for expansions of two elementary schools. This was a major triumph in a school system that was struggling financially. I told the guys about the unusual values code we had implemented for all pupils in grades K–12 and the new and improved discipline regulations that were now in place at all schools. And we had also increased the academic requirements for graduation from our senior high.

I emphasized that my staff was working very hard with cases of student substance abuse via a state-of-the-art intervention program. We had rescued many kids before they got too immersed in the drug scene. And we were getting pretty good at it.

I had lots of praise for my teaching staff. I had sat in literally hundreds of classrooms, and I almost always liked what I saw. Bubbly but polite kids on task with caring teachers! I accented our increasingly diverse student population as an asset, a source of pride for what our staff did each and every day with students. We had some of the largest schools in the Greater Philadelphia area, and yet my schools had a well-deserved reputation in our community for being very individualized and personal places. I knew this firsthand because I was regularly talking to students and parents in the Upper Darby community where I now lived. I went on and on.

And then Sal suddenly interrupted and dropped a bomb on me. "Joey, I don't get this. You're tellin' us all this good stuff and I don't doubt you know what you're talkin' about. But on radio and television and in the papers, all I ever read and hear and see is that public schools are cesspools with kids swingin' on chandeliers, ignoring their teachers, and learning little or nothing. I've seen Reagan's big shots, political humps from the state, and news media types by the score beatin' on the schools. If what you're tellin' us is true, then you guys in the school business have got a major credibility problem. Joey, you should be doin' somethin' to counter the bullshit flyin' around this country."

Leave it to Sal to be initiating a blunt discussion of politics and public education in the United States. And he couldn't have been more on target. Educational leaders in the public schools across America were much too complacent about the negative tide of public education criticism sweeping across the nation. And I was probably as guilty as the rest of my colleagues.

Our administrator heads were buried in the sands of handling the daily challenges in our schools while enemies were surrounding us. Too many of us were underestimating the problem while politically motivated Darth Vaders were lurking just outside, ready to pounce upon and destroy public education in America.

Sal, Rocco, Guido, and I went to the funeral and said goodbye to the last of a breed. Sal's dad was something else, a very benevolent godfather of the first order. A criminal, true, but with no drug trafficking in his repertoire of evil doing. Later on that day, my three old friends and I drank several gallons of homemade Italian red wine and toasted the dearly departed. Indeed, all us were now without fathers.

When we went our separate ways after the mourning, Sal's words of wisdom over breakfast burned on inside of me. I knew he was right. I spent the next few weeks researching the popular news media. I read four newspapers each day and watched a host of *Face the Nation*-type television shows. It was much worse than even I thought.

Years before, I had read Aldous Huxley's *Brave New World*. I found a dusty copy of the book amid my collection of treasured volumes and reread it. One of the fascinating aspects of *Brave New World* is hynopaedia. Although supposedly a fictional concept, I now saw hynopaedia as a tactic being used to manage and control the American public. One hundred repetitions three nights a week for four years . . . 62,400 repetitions will make anything into the truth.

What was happening on the national news media and what Sal had reacted to, undoubtedly like many other citizens across the country, was a hypnopaedia strategy. Public education bashers just kept telling the same lies about schooling in America over and over again. And now it was becoming truth!

One of the best books that documents this campaign of deception is *The Manufactured Crisis* by David Berliner and Bruce Biddle. Here's just a bit of what they wrote:

> The manufactured crisis myth about America's public schools has involved a serious campaign by identifiable persons to sell Americans the false idea that their public schools are failing and that because of this failure the nation was at peril. This campaign has involved a great deal of slimy effort, chicanery, playing on people's worries, pandering to prejudices, and misreporting and misrepresenting evidence.

CHAPTER 16

It is never easy to acknowledge that one is gullible—that one has swallowed deceptions sold by charlatans—and this is particularly hard when those deceptions are massive and from people with power. And yet, many goodhearted Americans have been victimized in just that way.

Exploding the Myths by Joe Schneider and Paul Houston is another work that summarizes the same type of exploitation of the masses with lies. Its authors write:

> As far as we're concerned, many of our political and corporate leaders are using educational reform as a scapegoat for problems that schools didn't cause and can't fix. We believe many of these elected leaders and their corporate sponsors are engaging in a conspiracy against candor with the American people regarding public education.

One of the best-known leaders of the anti-public education movement was William Bennett, ironically the secretary of education under President Ronald Reagan. Bennett's pompous diatribes against public schools were convincing. He was an intimidating speaker. And he ran wild in and on the American news media.

Frosty Troy, the publisher of the *Oklahoma Observer* and a staunch advocate of public education, offers this blunt summary of the Bennett impact in *Church and State* (October 1998):

> William Bennett, who never spent a day in his life in public education and has no background in the field, was appointed Secretary of Education by President Ronald Reagan. His instructions: shut down the United States Department of Education and do what he could to defund public schools at the federal level. Bennett relished the job, weeding out every pro-public education department official, and used his office as a bully pulpit to bash the public schools. His stewardship was so bad, the General Accounting Office did a special audit citing his abject failure as an administrator.... He has produced more false messages against public education than any other living American.

William Bennett, of course, has had lots of prestigious company over the years. Jerry Falwell, Pat Robertson, Lamar Alexander, Newt Gingrich, Rush Limbaugh, and many corporate CEOs have each expended significant efforts trying to discredit public education. It's been a masterful propaganda onslaught for almost twenty years now.

Back in the 1980s, the most amazing phenomenon was the ineptitude of the response from the public education establishment to all the lies and deceit being spread about the schools. And yet the credibility and integrity of the institution in which we worked was being seriously questioned. If people stopped believing in public education, nothing good that happened inside those schools would matter. Propagandists would prevail, and public education would be doomed. Superintendents should have been in the forefront of this fight. Unfortunately, too many of my colleagues were missing in action.

For some, it was just a matter of apathy. For others, it was a more myopic view. No time to do battle at the national level. Too many things to get done in their own trenches. And for many of my white, male, upper-middle-class colleagues, it was a matter of political reality. Many of them lived in Republican fiefdoms: "Challenge the White House Royal King, Ronald Reagan? What're you, crazy? I could lose my job! So what's coming out of the Republican White House about public schools is asinine! I'm not getting involved!"

And yet, as I flew on airplanes, watched television, listened to radio, or just attended a social event, the same message was being propagandized everywhere: "Public schools are a disaster; failing their students and the nation." Except in my everyday experience, this just wasn't the case!

All of this was very disillusioning. Where was the moral outrage within my own profession? Where was the sense of conviction? Where was courage to fight back? I despaired. Life is much too short for school leaders to wallow in the shadow of cautious insignificance and resultant invisibility. It was The Silence of the Shepherds!

THE INSANITY SPEECH

My predecessor and mentor Mike once told me that when you really care about something and you want something to happen, act like a madman. His strategy seemed to fit the needs of the late 1980s and early 1990s. There was a message that people needed to hear. And I was more than a little crazy. Perhaps the public would listen to a mad scientist more than they would to a school superintendent.

I wrote a tongue-in-cheek speech in which I documented my many hours of medical research laboring feverishly in the darkness of my office laboratory. The scenario was that I had isolated and analyzed three diseases pervading America. Truly, the fallacies and irrationalities and outright lies of so many governmental and corporate leaders about public education were an indication that their minds had been poisoned by the pervasive mental illnesses I had discovered.

Like any good Nobel Prize winner, I unveiled my three newly discovered diseases:

- **Perverted Distortionism:** A disease of organizations and individuals bent on destroying public schools. Many of those afflicted are right-wing extremists who would impose their sectarian beliefs on everyone. Still others are infected by their conviction that public education is some government plot to destroy organized religion and the American family. These divinely inspired souls believe that they have the

CHAPTER 17

monopoly on their version of God who directs their efforts. And finally, some people with this illness are delirious with the idea of privatizing the public schools to make tons of money.

- **Quantification Syndrome:** The fever most affecting state governors and even presidents of the United States as well as a host of other elected officials who think that you fatten the cattle by weighing them over and over again. The sad effect of this hallucinatory disease is that U.S. students are already the most overtested in the world. And the tragedy is that all of those billions of dollars spent for testing could be so much better utilized for teaching and learning and enrichment initiatives.
- **Simple Simonitis:** A most serious brain disorder that has infected people from all walks of life in every corner of America. And for some strange reason, corporate executives are especially vulnerable. This illness causes its victims to see public schools in a vacuum. These persons pretend to not have any idea of the societal turbulence that is altering American culture—the drugs, lawlessness, poverty, materialism, and valueless heroes surrounding our young people. Meanwhile, while money drives everything in the private sector, for public schools, money is never the answer. Illogic rules!

I initially tried out this speech on a friendly audience of middle school educators at a large state conference. Of course, I elaborated at length on the three diseases, naming names, citing examples, and taking no prisoners, speaking for about twenty minutes. Five minutes into the address, the audience finally realized I wasn't an institutional escapee. They caught on to the fact that I was conveying a very serious message. When I finished, the appreciative teachers and school administrators gave me a standing ovation. It encouraged me to carry my medical research to the multitudes.

I next delivered my Insanity Speech to a select committee of elected officials gathering data on public education reform. I spoke as a citizen of the Commonwealth, even though I was invited to address the committee because I was a school superintendent. At first, I figured this group was not very bright. Perhaps they thought I had a few screws loose. They just listened to me with glazed over eyes. I speculated for a moment that they didn't get it. But, no, they got it all right. Especially the parts about government of-

THE INSANITY SPEECH

ficials being obsessed with standardized testing programs as the ultimate magic wand for public schools. These politicians were seething. They responded to the end of my speech with stony silence!

My next speaking adventure was to an audience of school board members from many different school districts in Pennsylvania. My Insanity Speech provoked the group. In the question-and-answer period, some school directors proclaimed me to be an idiot. In contrast, other attendees evaluated my prepared remarks as brilliant. There were some skirmishes between persons in the audience. It was great fun. There was some yelling and screaming. So nice to see everyone involved in an intellectual discussion. At least I wasn't boring.

When I finally departed the room, one red-faced school board–type from rural Pennsylvania was being restrained from coming after me. It turned out he was a medical doctor. He had gone ballistic when I quoted an ABC news report on the United States' very high infant mortality rates among industrialized nations around the world. I was making the analogy that this "test score on infant mortality" could be unilaterally utilized to evaluate the American medical establishment as a colossal failure. I was just baiting the audience to make a point. Measuring quality can rarely be accomplished with a simple quantitative indicator that does not take into account all the variables impacting the situation in question. Just putting the shoe on the other foot for once. And judging by this physician's reaction, it certainly proved the point.

My Insanity Speech launched my career as a radical. I became a troublemaker. I was outspoken and often confrontational, supposedly not good for the image of an educational leader. This was a dangerous pathway for my career as a school superintendent. I didn't care! In subsequent years, I carried many out-of-the-mainstream messages in support of public education to the friendly and the hostile, the conservative and the liberal, the corporate and the plebeian. It was hardly for fun. But it mattered. And at least some day in the future when I'm on my deathbed, I won't have to wish I had stood up and taken a stand for what I believed.

18

THE PRIVATE SECTOR AND THE SCHOOLS

In 1983, the National Commission on Excellence in Education created an onslaught of public school bashing with its report entitled *A Nation at Risk*. The central idea of this work was that public schools were unilaterally responsible for the struggling U.S. economy of the early 1980s. Within just a few years, that same message was being regularly endorsed by think tanks, universities, television evangelists, and many private sector sources. All hell broke loose. The credibility of public education was decimated.

Many alleged experts growing very long noses were preaching this sermon of untruth. Talking heads and the news media in general did wonders in spreading the propaganda. In this scenario, the stock market downturns were directly related to the quality of the inferior public schools in the United States. International business and industry competitors from Asia and Europe were besting American competitor companies for one reason— our public schools just weren't getting the job done!

Ironically, throughout the 1990s, as I heard this garbage repeated over and over, U.S. corporations battled back to the top of world competitiveness. Our stock market once again became bullish year after year. The Asian dollar had a meltdown while the European economy struggled to survive. Wait a minute here. I respectfully request a retraction!

In the simplistic logic of these public education bashers, the majority of whom were business executives and high-level government officials, if American schooling was condemned because of the downturned economy of the

CHAPTER 18

early 1980s, then because of the booming, successful American economy during the 1990s, public schools should have received great praise and adulation. But there was only silence from the private sector as events turned and remained better economically. That's because this argument was always flawed.

Correlating the ups and downs of the U.S. economy with the quality of public schools is blatantly absurd. The perpetrators of these lies knew it all along. It was a deliberate campaign of deceit against the American public and a vile crime against public education. For when the economy had gone sour, those most vocal critics of public schools from the private sector and government were covering up for their own lack of competence in that very competitive international market.

Lawrence Cremin, writing in *Popular Education and Its Discontents*, makes this argument:

> American economic competitiveness with Japan and other nations is to a considerable degree a function of monetary, trade, and industrial policy, and of decisions made by the President, the Congress, the Federal Reserve Board, and the departments of the Treasury and Commerce and Labor. To contend that the problems of international competitiveness can be solved by reforming schools is not merely utopian but millennialist. It is at best foolish and at worst it is a crass effort to direct attention away from those truly responsible for doing something about competitiveness and to lay the burden instead on the schools.

In short, far beyond the classroom walls of public schools, policies of the federal government, trade laws, tariffs, export and import strategies, and the quality of top management corporate decision making are the true factors in international economic competition. And when things weren't going well in the marketplace, it just became an convenient strategy of governmental and private sector leaders to slander public education as the culprit.

On another attack front during the 1990s, many corporate CEOs have chastised public schools for not creating the necessary workers with high-tech skills and problem-solving abilities that corporations need. In the forefront has been IBM president Louis Gerstner, one of the latest national spokespersons for public education improvement, with his own book out on the topic.

But Clinton Boutwell, writing in *Shell Game,* documents some serious contradictions about this newest savior of education:

> Gertsner's own executive behavior belied the message of his book. IBM made its reputation, and huge profits, by employing the high-tech researchers, engineers, and technical developers who represented the finest products of American schools, indeed the very kind of graduates Gertsner claimed schools are not supplying to business. Yet, in line with IBM's new "lean and mean" management strategy, Gertsner fired 90,000 of those highly trained employees, just about one third of IBM's 270,000 employees. That was in addition to the other 183,000 quality employees that IBM fired before Gertsner arrived.

Tragically, Gerstner has not been alone. In fact, his behavior was rather typical. While so many of America's 1990s private sector rhetoricians were pontificating similar arguments to Gerstner's about not getting quality workers from public schools, corporations were simultaneously rolling heads by the hundreds of thousands. Xerox, AT&T, Bank of America, United Technologies, General Motors, Sears ... the list goes on and on. In summary, this bloodletting was the height of corporate hypocrisy.

Ironically, in the midst of this private sector debacle, one favorite theme of the corporate education bashers was that money is not the answer: "Public schools are in trouble," they proposed, "but government shouldn't just be throwing dollars at the schools. These schools should be more fiscally responsible, run with the wonderful efficiencies of the private sector which would never operate with government handouts." What a crock!

An investigative story in the *Philadelphia Inquirer* (June 4, 1995) painted a much different picture than the creative rhetoric of the pious private sector. From 1990 to 1994, the federal government handed out $293 million to eight major U.S. corporations (Amoco, AT&T, Citicorp, DuPont, General Electric, General Motors, IBM, and Motorola) to stimulate business. The travesty of this corporate welfare was that those eight corporations in 1994 alone already had profits of $26 billion! And even with this taxpayer handout, the eight cited corporations cut more than 300,000 jobs from 1990 to 1994. Three of the eight wonder companies (Amoco, DuPont, and General Electric) actually cut their research and development programs from 1990 to 1994 in spite of the government's giveaway.

CHAPTER 18

This is not a pretty picture. When I think of federal charity for rich corporations, I am repulsed. In a nation with millions of children living below the poverty line, that money could have worked wonders with our most impoverished schools.

What all of this comes down to is that public education needs no lectures about reform from the private sector. Corporate America has enough of its own problems. A most recent example is the Enron scandal. This giant American business created an illusion of success with a host of shell partnerships. Debt was well hidden. And while Enron's executives profited from this scam, the company's demise was inevitable. Shredded documents and influence peddling at the highest levels of our government were in this mix. Eventually, Enron's workers and stockholders went down the drain. So spare me the sermons, please!

In summary, I have long ago rejected the private sector's manipulations and hypocritical con games regarding public education. And I still bleed for America's poor when I think of corporate game playing and incestuous relationships of the private sector with government. For too many powerful American corporations, the public schools have been a very useful target, a convenient distraction of the public's attention away from corporate corruption and private sector welfare. And what more perverse use of public schools than as a cover-up for the mediocre and sometimes poor management decisions of corporate executives?

THE MORAL VACUUM

Working as a school superintendent through most of the 1990s was sort of like being trapped inside an insane asylum. So many of the serious issues facing public education across America were just sitting there being ignored by all levels of governmental leadership.

In the financial arena, very few prominent elected officials seemed (or is it wanted?) to notice that there was a growing disparity in the quality of public education from community to community based on the wealth of each school community. Far too many politicians simply denied the fact that the most important factor in determining the scope and quality of educational offerings in any school system was the extent of financial resources in that community.

There was a sick rationale for all of this. To posit the government's role in equalizing educational opportunities for all students requires true belief in the highest American ideals and principles. However, translating such conviction into reality also demands significant financial appropriations. Forget about ideals and principles. This was politics!

After all, in finest American tradition, it's always been better to pretend. And it does take courage to take a hard look at our national societal landscape. Certainly, there are many public schools across the United States that educate basically homogenous student populations amidst affluent community surroundings. But there are also numerous public schools servicing large numbers of educationally disadvantaged pupils from very im-

CHAPTER 19

poverished areas. Many of these schools are barely surviving in terms of relative educational resources. And there are a host of middle-of-the-road schools that must educate very heterogeneous student bodies without an adequate tax base to support their schools. It is the role of an enlightened government to remedy such unevenness.

Unfortunately, too many of our elected princes and princesses live and work in wonderful kingdoms far away from the everyday world. For the most part, they operate inside their palatial environs. And then every once in a while, these royal leaders come outside to profess their deep commitment for education to the American citizenry. Many of these politicians speak about equity among public schools as if it were an American reality rather than an American fantasy.

At one time, I might have believed that a free press, our fourth estate, would protect our citizenry from governmental hypocrisy, naiveté, and inaction. However, during much of my career as a school superintendent, most of the news media were in deep hibernation, sleeping through their obligations to an informed public. The working press were too apathetic, too negative, and too simplistic to make a positive difference for public education or the American people.

Okay, so maybe I'm over the deep end. More than a few politicians have told me that I'm a looney tune. I really can't imagine why! I just have a few concerns. And I can't find anyone to address them.

First, how is it possible that millions of children in the United States attend schools that are in need of repair or renovation? Tragically, the American Society of Civil Engineers has found that schools, more than any other part of this nation's infrastructure (highways, bridges, drinking water and waste disposal facilities, etc.), are in the most need of repair. One-third of the public schools across the United States have at least one major problem (e.g., leaky roofs or crumbling walls). And one-half of America's schools are beset with difficulties such as inadequate plumbing, poor heating, and lighting problems.

In a society where just about every elected official boasts about his or her deep commitment to children and schooling, how can this be? Local communities are doling out about $20 billion each year trying to keep up with school facilities improvements, but that is far from solving the problem. The federal government also needs to get more involved.

THE MORAL VACUUM

The National School Boards Association notes in one of its 2001 Advocacy Position Papers that the General Accounting Office has estimated that more than $110 billion is currently needed to meet the school facility needs crisis in the nation. So many deteriorating school buildings and so many others in need of modernization should certainly be a cause for concern in Washington, D.C. It is in fact a national crisis and federal government action (dollars) is a required part of the solution here. In our initiatives for educational improvement, an obvious first step is to ensure that our school buildings across America are structurally sound learning environments for our children.

Second, America has been and continues to be plagued by uneven, inequitably funded basic education schemes for schools. Largely a deliberate malfunction of state politicians, there have been numerous disaster stories of inadequate financial support of public schools, especially for those with the most impoverished children.

Spin doctors working for legislatures and governors have had marvelous success in confusing and conning the general public. The state commits the crime of inadequately funding public education and then blames the victim, the schools. The news media buy in. It's an old scam that still works very well today, especially for politicians.

In Pennsylvania, the decade of the 1990s under the administrations of Democrat Robert Casey and Republican Thomas Ridge was devoid of any moral commitment to equitably funding public schools. The Casey administration, with a legislative majority controlled by its party, removed a model funding formula (Equalized Subsidy for Basic Education) in the early 1990s to save money at the state level. Hundreds of public schools across Pennsylvania were now underfunded each year while numerous state politicians bragged about their fiscal prowess in generating conservatively responsible Commonwealth budgets.

In subsequent years, the Ridge administration stayed the course. Way back in 1974-75, Pennsylvania government actually paid a 50% share of the statewide costs of basic instruction in public schools. But by the year 2000, after Casey and Ridge had finished with their mischief, Pennsylvania was paying only a 37% share of the overall basic instructional costs of its public schools. This was the most ignored news story in the history of newspapers. And it's hard to understand why!

CHAPTER 19

Maybe it's because for many upper-class, white, homogenized school communities, state subsidies for public schools didn't matter that much. They had the rich local real estate tax bases to offset the underfunding by the state.

For my own Upper Darby School District, serving one of the most densely populated communities in Pennsylvania, with a rapidly growing student population and with a declining real estate tax base, the results of lessening annual state subsidies drove local property taxes through the roof. Likewise, for urban school systems in the Commonwealth, many already having very high real estate tax rates, not receiving their full share of state funding was a financial disaster year after year.

What happened in the city of Philadelphia is one of the most vivid illustrations of this state villainy. In 1999, the superintendent of schools, David Hornbeck, after several years of frustration with arbitrary funding from the Commonwealth, refused to make any further cuts in educational programs in the school system and even accused Pennsylvania's government of having racist motives.

The School District of Philadelphia was now headed for a financial crash! Hornbeck was probably trying to shame the state into action with his comments. He had good reason. Philadelphia's per-pupil spending ranked well below almost all of its suburban neighbors. And the city's urban population of largely minority students was the biggest loser during those Casey and Ridge years when the state was paying its lessening share of school funding to its 500-plus school districts each year.

Hornbeck's remarks essentially signed his own death warrant. Thou shalt not be confrontational with state royalty. It was not practical to challenge Pennsylvania's politically ambitious Governor Ridge and his Republican legislature. Forget about the moral imperatives for some of Pennsylvania's most needy students. Hornbeck was put on the political hit list in Harrisburg. Shortly thereafter, he was history. Hornbeck's departure was the outcome of a bipartisan deal between state and Philadelphia politicians for thirty pieces of silver, a one-time shot of survival funding from the Commonwealth to keep Philadelphia's schools from going under. Pennsylvania politics at their usual worst.

And it wasn't just Philadelphia that suffered during this money crisis. The abdication of its funding responsibilities for public education over so many years has fiscally brutalized many other Commonwealth school systems. The Pennsylvania School Boards Association has documented the fact that one billion dollars has been imposed by local school boards on the real estate tax base in communities across the Commonwealth to offset this lack of funding from the state. And this has created a backlash reaction against public education by a host of local taxpayer groups who attack their school boards and vilify their community's schools.

Through these difficult times, those of us who worked in school systems were always told by the state bureaucracy that we needed to tighten our fiscal management belts. But that cliché was only for public schools. State politicians could always find plenty of money for their true political priorities. Public education just wasn't one of them throughout the 1990s.

From the federal government, the hypocrisy was just as bad. In 1975, the Congress of the United States passed sweeping legislation for individuals with disabilities to have full access to all of the benefits of the public education system. The congressional commitment was to fund the new law's requirements at a 40% level. But then whoever said that there was honor among politicians?

Over the twenty-five-year period from the inception of the Individuals with Disabilities Education Act (IDEA) legislation, the American Association of School Administrators has estimated that the federal government has shortchanged local school districts more than $300 billion in their provision of services to special education needs students. That's because the Congress never came anywhere near funding at the 40% share it had indicated it would provide.

For example, for the year 2000, a 40% share of federal funding to all school districts nationwide for providing services under the IDEA would have amounted to $15.8 billion; but the federal government appropriated only $4.9 billion. This left local school districts across the nation holding the bill for an extra $10.9 billion just in the year 2000. This was an incredible drain on local resources to fund a strictly enforced federal mandate.

To make this more clear, prior to the IDEA, the average share of school district budgets across the country that was devoted to regular (basic) education hovered around 80%. By 1996, with year after year of inadequate funding from the federal government for IDEA, the average percentage of school budgets dedicated to regular education all across America had

CHAPTER 19

dropped under 60%. All of this is a very sad commentary on the Congress of the United States and its breach of promise to public schools and special needs children.

My third concern is an unfortunate portrait of how our government really works. The Associated Press reported in the *Philadelphia Inquirer* (July 9, 1998) that in 1997, 14,484 lobbyists worked the U.S. Senate and House of Representatives on behalf of their special interests. In that year, lobbyists outnumbered members of Congress by a 27-1 ratio. I had always wondered why Congress had such a deaf ear and blind eye to addressing the real issues in American education. And now I had my answer. Just in 1997, these corporate and private sector advocates spent $1.17 billion to swing elected officials over to their causes. Who says money doesn't matter? Especially when you're a legislator filling up your coffers with lobbyist money and perks.

In the midst of all of this, elected officials and corporate leaders continue to this day to act remarkably naive regarding the challenges of public schools. Small wonder. Within the context of our class-layered society in the United States, advantaged people have little knowledge or concern for the underprivileged. But public schools, more than any other institution, have to deal with student bodies that reflect America's largely ignored set of demographics on a daily basis.

Marian Wright Edelman of the The Children's Defense Fund has issued this challenge to the Congress of the United States to make the right choices, morally and politically: "We have nothing to be proud of. One in six children in the United States—12.1 million—still live in poverty. In fact, children are more likely to be poor today in this time of unprecedented wealth than they were 20 to 30 years ago. Nearly eleven million are without health insurance." The need for public schools to address a host of social service issues as well as providing preschool education and enrichment resources is enormous. Our federal government badly needs a wake up call. Ms. Edelman continues: "We must make significant efforts to lift children and their families out of poverty. We have the know-how, the experience, the tools, and the resources to end child poverty and suffering. And we have the responsibility as mothers, fathers, grandparents and concerned and sensible citizens to act now!"

Added to the issue of poverty in America, the Census Bureau has revealed that the ethnic diversity of America's children continues to increase. Only 64% of our young people are now white, non-Hispanic. The largest foreign-born populations in the United States are in rank order from Mexico, the Philippines, Vietnam, Cuba, China, India, El Salvador, the Dominican Republic, Canada, and Korea. The vast majority of children from these families attend public schools. Most of these youngsters are far from wealthy. These pupils present a unique set of needs to educators ranging from language barriers to vast cultural differences. Finally, more than 40 million Americans change addresses every year. This is a major problem for public school educators trying to effect sequential learning programs in their classrooms.

For many of these problems, money is the answer. And government needs to be a much more aggressive partner in closing the gaps between haves and have-nots in America. Public schools deserve and need help and support, not empty promises nor criticism.

In closing, since setting goals for public schools is a regularly heard echo in today's national landscape, I respectfully submit that politicians and government leaders should also have a set of measurable objectives, so here they are:

- Every politician who wishes to speak about public education must first provide proof of having been inside a public school in a nonaffluent community for a series of meaningful visits to classrooms as well as for conversations with administrators, teachers, students, and parents.
- All legislation in the future must be addressed to the needs of students as defined by people with experience inside public schools, not by political party agendas.
- All elected officials must begin to use their own brains when thinking about public education, rather than listening to biased think tanks, vested interests attempting to privatize public schools, or religious fundamentalists seeking to funnel money to private and parochial schools.
- Elected officials will abandon their mandates for superfluous standardized testing programs and spend that money for an educational agenda for America's school students.
- The U.S. Congress will exhibit responsible leadership by financially addressing the needs of our vast underclass and educationally disadvantaged pupils.
- A standardized test will be administered to all elected officials to determine their grasp of the complex issues facing a system of public education

CHAPTER 19

valiantly trying to teach a tremendously diverse student body. Failure to obtain a passing grade will result in removal from office.

In summary, there has been too much hollow lip service paid to public education by government over too many years. It's time to move beyond simplistic standardized testing programs as panaceas for public schools. Its time to start listening to the people who work in the trenches about what public schools really need. And its time for America to finance the qualitative programs (universal preschool education, remedial and enrichment courses, school-based before- and after-school programs, professional staff development, technology initiatives, leadership training, school construction and building modernization support, fair share special education funding, and smaller class sizes) in public schools that will make the difference for all children.

AN AUTHOR UNPUBLISHED

My father was a factory worker for more than thirty-five years. As I was growing up and until I reached about fourteen years of age, my dad and I were pretty close. He loved to get up early and cook breakfast and drink lots of coffee before he headed off to work. I was usually there with him in the kitchen each and every day. I relished those mornings. Just a father and his son. We had wonderful discussions. From world events to local politics to religion to music and art and sports, the maintenance man would philosophize to his son, frequently moralizing and drawing life lessons for me from whatever we talked about. On those mornings, my dad spoke to me with animation and passion and principle. And many of his messages and the life priorities he emphasized are still part of my moral foundation today.

And then about the time I entered high school, my father abruptly switched personalities. He still never missed a day of work and he was doing his thing in the kitchen every morning, but suddenly he became very sullen and withdrawn. The morning discussions stopped. My dynamic philosopher father had disappeared. When I tried to perk him up, he just stared ahead, sometimes teary-eyed. From that point forward, he became very quiet and spoke very little. The eloquent preacher who held court with me as his only audience on so many mornings was gone.

In 1980, my father died. A few days after the funeral, I was at our old row house in Philly having lunch with my mother. I wanted some lasting momento of my father. She told me that I could scavenge around the basement

CHAPTER 20

and look through the hundreds of cardboard boxes in storage there. She really didn't know what was there because she hardly ever went down into the basement anymore.

I had to get back to work in the nearby Upper Darby School District, but I had a few minutes. In the cellar I pushed aside some piles of junk, and then I found a box filled with of all things, my father's writing. Dad had always told me that he could have been a writer. But I never took any of this seriously. Why should I? For all the years that I had known him, my father was a maintenance man in a factory. However, be not so quick to judge. For in life, you never know what someone might become and you never know what they might have been. And what was in this cardboard box was astounding.

I read through some beautiful love letters from my father to my mother from back in the depression years. I was astonished! I perused what appeared to be a handwritten speech in which my father as a union official in the factory was proclaiming that he was not a Red (communist).

And then I hit gold. I found a double-spaced typewritten short story authored by my father back in the 1930s. It had supernatural overtones as the devil claimed a lost soul by tossing the body of a sinful victim into the path of an oncoming subway train. Lots of crisp dialogue and as chilling a plot as you could want. I was flabbergasted! For someone living in a company (coal mining) town just outside Wilkes Barre (PA) in the middle of the depression, the short story was a magnificent accomplishment by my father.

Attached to the ten-page short story was a copy of my father's letter to a major magazine publisher asking for consideration of his piece of writing. Affixed to that cover letter was the polite rejection response from the publisher. And there was one more attachment. A copy of my father's short story in print with somebody else's name listed as the author.

My mind pieced it all together in seconds. Forty some years prior to his death, my father had in fact been a budding writer. When he tried to make the leap into the professional arena, his short story creation had been blatantly stolen from him. I can't know for sure, but this was likely the end of his writing career. Sue someone? People from his social class in his environment hardly knew what lawyers were, let alone were able to pay for one. So much for dreams. Dad and my mom moved to the urbanity of Philadelphia for the lucrative riches of working in a factory.

I wasn't sure exactly what I was going to do with my father's writing samples, if anything. For the time being, I was already one hour past the time I was supposed to return to work. I put everything neatly back into its cardboard box container and exited the basement. I told my mother that I had in fact found a box with some of my father's stuff. I would return next week to get what I wanted.

Two days later, my mother called me at the school district to tell me about her most recent adventure. As usual, Mom had handled adversity by taking care of everything herself. No need to bother me. She told me that the day after my most recent visit a broken water pipe had sent four feet of water into her basement. It was quite some time before she thankfully discovered the problem. Not to worry though. The plumbers were wonderful, repairing the pipes, draining the water, shoveling out the resultant mud, and carting away piles of soaking wet cardboard and paper that had been floating around the cellar. My mother wanted to assure me though that my father's box of tools was not harmed by the flood. Was that what I had wanted?

Well, Dad, now that you're gone I think I understand more about you than I ever imagined. You deserved a chance as a writer and never got it. I know... I know... you always told me that life isn't fair. But geez, Dad! Anyway, this book is for *you*. It was inspired in me by you, an unpublished writer. I hope that wherever you are, you enjoy it very much.

EPILOGUE

The Bywood Elementary School is a wondrous place. Located on the east side of the Upper Darby School District just a mile or so from the Philadelphia border, it houses a very heterogeneous population of more than 800 students in grades one through five.

The school is a gentle and caring refuge in the heart of a densely populated community. Its children are of many different colors and religions. A wide range of socioeconomic backgrounds are represented in the pupil population. And the languages spoken in the homes of students number well over twenty. Bywood students tend to excel academically as they move on in the school system. Each year, its former students are as well represented among Upper Darby High School's highest academic achievers as those from any other elementary school in the district.

Joey always cherished Bywood. He enjoyed roaming its halls to watch the school's dedicated teachers in action with their kids. The culture of the place was love. It was the way American schooling was supposed to be. A school working daily miracles with a student population with a myriad of needs.

Joey had retired as Upper Darby's school superintendent in 1999. But now on November 14, 2001, he was back on Bywood's concrete campus for the school's senior prom. Bywood's prom is not to be confused with high school events similarly named. After all Bywood is an elementary school, and in this case, senior means senior citizen.

Here's what was about to happen. Under the direction of the school's masterfully talented music teacher Maryanne, the Bywood Buddies, a

EPILOGUE

marvelous student performing group, were going to entertain hundreds of senior citizen visitors from the Upper Darby area with a short concert. And then the pupils would proceed to spend the rest of the afternoon dancing the hours away with their much older guests.

Joey was seated in the Bywood gymnasium, waiting for the festivities to begin. The place was colorfully decorated. The gym was jammed with seniors, many of whom volunteered regularly in Bywood's classrooms. Some of the older citizens had even dressed up as clowns to add a joyous dimension to the day. The Bywood Buddies were up front, decked out in white gloves and shirts with green jazzbows and matching cummerbunds. The children began demonstrating their mastery of vocal excellence. They sang like angels. Their smiling faces and innocence brought tears to many of the older faces, including Joey's. It was all very moving. It was what he came for!

And then the disc jockey began the music. Nine- and ten-year-old youngsters were suddenly paired up doing the jitterbug with people who had lived through World War II. Amidst a dance floor filled with intergenerational couples, Joey was demonstrating some South Philly dance moves to his partner, a tiny Vietnamese American fifth-grader who had very politely asked him to dance. It was all a beautiful happening.

The music switched to disco. Joey opted for a breather and some punch and headed for the food tables. He bumped smack into one of the senior citizens dressed as a clown and apologized. Then Joey looked into this clown's eyes and saw something very familiar.

"No need to be sorry, Joey! It's only me!" So spoke Guido's deep voice from underneath his spiked red hair, oversized purple nose, and painted green lips. My God, this clown was Guido! Joey nearly had a coronary on the spot.

Guido continued: "You weren't kiddin,' Joey. Everything you've been tellin' us for years about this school and its kids is true. That's why Sal and Rocco and me came out to see for ourselves today. They're breakin' our hearts." Sal and Rocco were here? Joey gasped for air and looked nervously around the floor full of dancers.

And sure enough, on the other side of the gymnasium, Joey spotted Sal and Rocco animatedly holding court with coffee and cake in hand amidst a group of senior citizens seated at one of the many tables. For a moment, Joey was apprehensive. What if some fifth-graders ask them to dance? And then

EPILOGUE

suddenly Joey grew very embarrassed at himself. He chastised himself for being an elitist fool, for forgetting where he came from and who his real friends were.

So what was so wrong about any of this, anyway? This party was for senior citizens. Guido, Sal, and Rocco all qualified. They had in fact retired from their business. And as a matter of fact, when that happened Sal had proudly bought memberships for all of his guys in AARP. More important, Sal and Rocco and Guido had cared enough to come to a prom that was a very important lifeblood event for the children of Bywood School.

A tall African American fifth-grader asked Joey to do the twist with her. He readily complied and got badly outclassed as a dancer. Joey then rock and rolled through the next three numbers with three different kids. He needed to take a rest. Joey sat down, watched the room full of dancers, and just smiled. Sal and Rocco were now out on the floor dancing with fifth-grade partners. Guido was doing his clown thing all over the room. Joey was with his true friends doing something that truly mattered in a place he truly loved. Senior citizens and happy children and old friends bonded together. Life couldn't be any better than this.

A SUMMARY OF THE MESSAGES OF THIS BOOK

1. Too many educators don't pay enough attention to eliminating bullyism, that despicable practice of student hoodlums who prey on the weak or the different in our schools.
2. Mediocre teachers are validators. They take students as they come to them, label them, quantify them, and endorse their background/baggage with an appropriate grade that defines the pupils' worth. In contrast, great teachers are somehow able to effect positive change in all the students who come to them, no matter what problems or lack of skills they bring with them. Great teachers don't squash dreams; they build them.
3. Being a teacher is so much more than just directing the learning activities in a classroom. It's also being a surrogate parent, a counselor, and a missionary.
4. Always look for opportunity in the midst of adversity.
5. School public relations is hardly something dirty. It's telling the public what you're doing in the schools and why! It's also doing a good job and then publicizing it. And it's a critical necessity in the business of public education.
6. It's not *what* you do in public sector management. It's *how* you do it that really makes the difference.
7. Sometimes you punt the football and hope for the best. Smart administrators know when to punt.

A SUMMARY OF THE MESSAGES OF THIS BOOK

8. The most important asset for a superintendent is a caring heart.
9. An effective superintendent of schools is first and foremost a philosopher.
10. The hard reality is that a superintendent of schools functions under a public microscope. Educational leaders should dance under the magnifying glass rather than trying to shun it. Being a superintendent of schools involves highly visible missionary work, spiritual conviction, spreading a gospel, and converting others in the most visible of environments.
11. School board–administration relationships are often what the superintendent makes of them.
12. By the nature of the job, a superintendent of schools needs a special someone. The superintendency is not something you want to face alone.
13. In school administration, you're only as good as your next crisis. Tomorrow always brings new challenges and problems to overcome.
14. High-stakes standardized-test bludgeoning has no place in American education.
15. Always believe in angels. Always have faith in the goodness of caring people.
16. Life is much too short for school leaders to wallow in the shadow of cautious insignificance and resultant invisibility.
17. Measuring quality can rarely be accomplished with a simple quantitative indicator that does not take into account all the variables impacting upon the situation in question.
18. For many powerful American corporations, the public schools have been a very easy target, a convenient distraction of the public's attention away from corporate welfare, and a scapegoat to cover up the inadequacies of mediocre management decisions.
19. Many politicians speak about equity among public schools as if it were an American reality rather than an American fantasy.
20. Be not so quick to judge. For in life you never know what someone might become nor what they might have been.

BIBLIOGRAPHY

"A Conversation with Kozol." *The School Administrator*. Vol. 57, No. 10: November 2000 (p. 17).

Boston, Rob. "The Public School Bashers." *Church and State*. Vol. 51, No 9: October 1998 (p. 10).

Census 2000, United States Census Bureau. Washington, DC, 2000.

Berliner, David C., and Bruce J. Biddle. *The Manufactured Crisis*. Reading, MA: Addison-Wesley, 1995 (p. 9).

"Big Blue's White Elephant Sale," *Business Week*, 20 February 1995 (p. 36).

Boutwell, Clinton E. *Shell Game*. Bloomington, IN: Phi Delta Kappa, 1997 (pp. 9-10).

Cremin, Lawrence A. *Popular Education and Its Discontents*. New York: Harper & Row, 1989 (p. 103).

Edelman, Marian Wright. Testimony before Congressional Budget Committee. The Children's Defense Fund, August 8, 2001.

Gaul, Gilbert M., and Stranahan, Susan Q. "How Billions in Taxes Failed to Create Jobs." *The Philadelphia Inquirer*. June 4, 1995 (pp. A1 and A20).

Huxley, Aldous. *Brave New World*. New York: Harper and Row, 1946.

Kozol, Jonathan. Letter to *Education Week*. Vol. XXI, No. 11: November 14, 2001 (p. 37).

"Report Card on America's Infrastructure." Position Paper. Reston, VA: The American Society of Civil Engineers, 2001.

Salani, Jonathan D. "Interest Groups Spent $1.7 Billion to Lobby in D.C." *The Philadelphia Inquirer*. July 9, 1998 (p. E9).

Schneider, Joe, and Paul Houston. *Exploding the Myths*. Washington, DC: American Association of Education Service Agencies, 1993 (p. 3).

"School Construction and Renovation." Advocacy Position Paper. Alexandria, VA: National School Boards Association, 2001.

ABOUT THE AUTHOR

Joe Batory was the Upper Darby (PA) School District's Superintendent of Schools from 1984 to 1999 when he retired. He has been recognized for his numerous accomplishments as a public school leader with the Distinguished Lifetime Service Award from the American Association of School Administrators (2000). Additionally, in 1990, he was named as one of The Executive Educator 100, a group of only 100 outstanding school leaders chosen from America's 300,000 school administrators by a distinguished panel of independent jurors, all expert in the field.

Batory was cited with the Pennsylvania Music Educators' 1997 Superintendent of the Year award for his outstanding support of music programs in public schools. He has also received the 1998 Friend of Journalism award from the Pennsylvania School Press Association.

His service to children has been recognized with other awards from the Rotary Club of Upper Darby (1999 and 1989), the Delaware County Chamber of Commerce (1999), the Study Councils of the University of Pennsylvania (1999), the Delaware County Intermediate Unit (1999), the Patriotic Order of Sons of America (1992), the Upper Darby Teachers' Association (1999), Transport Workers Union Local 289 (1999), the Upper Darby Administrators and Supervisors Association (1999), the Upper Darby Educational Support Personnel (1999), the Drexel Hill Baptist Church (1999), and the National School Public Relations Association (1989).